C000263797

Animal Day

Pressure Testing The Martial Arts

Geoff Thompson

SUMMERSDALE

First published 1995.

This edition copyright © Geoff Thompson 2000

All rights reserved. The right of Geoff Thompson to be identified as the author of this work has been asserted in accordance with the Copyright, Designs and Patents Act of 1988.

No part of this book may be reproduced by any means, nor translated into a machine language, without the written permission of the publisher.

Summersdale Publishers Ltd
46 West Street
Chichester
West Sussex
PO19 1RP
United Kingdom

www.summersdale.com

Printed and bound in Great Britain by
4edge Ltd, Hockley. www.4edge.co.uk

ISBN 1 84024 111 X

Important note

If you have or believe you may have a medical condition the techniques outlined in this book should not be attempted without first consulting your doctor. Some of the techniques in this book require a high level of fitness and suppleness and should not be attempted by someone lacking such fitness. The author and the publishers cannot accept any responsibility for any proceedings or prosecutions brought or instituted against any person or body as a result of the use or misuse of any techniques described in this book or any loss, injury or damage caused thereby.

About the author

Geoff Thompson has written over 20 published books and is known world wide for his autobiographical books *Watch My back, Bouncer* and *On The Door*, about his nine years working as a night club doorman. He holds the rank of 5th Dan black belt in Japanese karate, 1st Dan in Judo and is also qualified to senior instructor level in various other forms of wrestling and martial arts. He has several scripts for stage, screen and TV in development with Destiny Films.

He has published several articles for GQ magazine, and has also been featured in *FHM, Maxim, Arena, Front* and *Loaded* magazines, and has been featured many times on mainstream TV.

Geoff is currently a contributing editor for *Men's Fitness* magazine and self defence columnist for *Front*.

Contents

Foreword   6
Fairbairn and Sykes
By Pete Robins

Introduction   10

Chapter One   15
Why Pressure Test?

Chapter Two   19
Understanding Yourself

Chapter Three   42
Understanding Your Art

Chapter Four   55
An Introduction To The Inner Opponent

Chapter Five   63
The Progressive Pyramid

Chapter Six   65
Grappling

Chapter Seven   74
Punching

Chapter Eight   77
Kicking

Chapter Nine   80
Weapons

Chapter Ten   82
Combining Distances

Chapter Eleven   86
Animal Day

Epilogue   95

Foreword

Fairbairn and Sykes

By Pete Robins

The underlying theme of this book on *pressure testing* that you are about to read is introducing and retaining a sense of reality in training. I have been asked to comment on this aspect of combatives from a historical viewpoint. Pressure testing is an aspect that has been readily overlooked, misunderstood or simply ignored by many of today's instructors in the martial arts. This is quite understandable as it is a subject that brings home the sheer horror of a real fight. A horror that most of us would prefer to avoid.

Only people who have stood up to a real fight understand that technique alone is not enough. Technique for its own sake, no matter how technical or *advanced* it is, no matter how pretty or pure it is, will not necessarily win the day. Many martial arts practitioners are led to believe by their instructors that physical effort is sufficient and pay little heed to the mental side of the equation. Often the instructor knows no better, but he should. Whenever he links in self-defence with his description of his system, he should be aware of all that self-defence, or rather self-protection, entails.

It is instructors like the author of this book, Geoff Thompson and his partner in the *British Combat Association*, Peter Consterdine, who should be listened to whenever the subject of self-protection rears its ugly head. These two men know what they are talking about, know what they are teaching and have carried out what must rate as one of the most comprehensive studies in our time of the least understood and talked about factors of fighting.

They are following the footsteps of two remarkable men who have been through a similar learning curve some 70 years ago. This empirical study had been carried out half way across the world in China. To be precise, Shanghai, famed as being in all probability the toughest city in the world. It was in the international settlement of this cosmopolitan city that W.E. Fairbairn, a member of the Shanghai police (SMP) from 1907 and E.A. ('Bill') Sykes, a police special from 1926, began their work together that has been recognised as the foundation of what we today term *Close Quarter Battle* (CQB).

These two men could not just rely on the theories about what might or might not occur in lethal encounters, they were dealing with harsh realities. They and fellow officers had to go into the myriad streets and alleyways, houses and opium dens that were the hideouts of their deadly enemy, to pursue the Chinese gangs that were the scourge of all Shanghai, and face these ruthless killers. What they found and knew was this: to face up to and survive a real encounter demanded nothing less and nothing more than simple and effective techniques. Methods that had been tried and tested. Any spurious or fancy manoeuvre would most likely fail and get them and their fellow officers maimed or killed. They honed and simplified their methods so that they could be taught to all the men of the SMP, not just the gifted few. They had to use techniques that could be retained under conditions of extreme stress. One might say extreme fear.

In all the training that Fairbairn set for the SMP in his role of chief instructor in self-defence - arrest and restraint, shooting, disarming, house-raids, bodyguard work and riot control techniques, he strove for a sense of realism. His men were *pressure tested* in all they did.

Animal Day

To give an example of his thoughts in that direction I refer to the findings in connection with actual shooting affrays that he and his men were involved in.

We go on to say that beyond helping to teach care in the handling of firearms, target shooting is of no value whatever in learning the use of the pistol as a weapon of combat . . . in the great majority of shooting affrays that distance at which firing takes place is not more than four yards, very frequently it is considerably less . . . It may happen that you have been running to overtake him. If you have had reason to believe that shooting is likely, you will be keyed up to the highest pitch and will be grasping your pistol with almost convulsive force. If you have to fire, your instinct will be to do so as quickly as possible, and you will probably do it with a bent arm, possibly even from the level of the hip . . . It may be that a bullet whizzes past you and that you will experience the momentary stupefaction which is due to the shock of the explosion at very short range of the shot just fired by your opponent - a very different feeling, we can assure you, from that experienced when you are standing behind or alongside a pistol that is being fired. (Shooting To Live)

Our sole concern is the use of the pistol as a fighting weapon. We have nothing to do with such matters as shooting with much pomp, ceremony and deliberation at passive black spots . . . Probably considerably more than eighty-five per cent of actual pistol fighting takes place at close quarters, in a hurry. Close quarters means anything from one yard to ten - it is difficult to define it more exactly. Hurry means a hell of a hurry - there is no difficulty in that definition. ('Bill' Sykes)

What they both knew was that the existing methods of shooting would in no way prepare men for actual combat conditions. What was taught in those days was target shooting which had no bearing at all on a shoot-out with an armed foe. There was no emphasis on speed, movement, lighting problems and the all important element - stress. Both knew the fear that hit a man at a time of grave danger, the surge of adrenalin that played havoc with the physical and mental system. Both knew that when danger *bursts through the door*, fancy technique and guesswork theories *fly out of the window*.

Fairbairn and Sykes understood that target shooting was to score points and was for recreation; combat shooting was for winning and for staying alive. The former cannot take the place of the latter. So they geared the training towards realism, to put as much pressure as was possible on the trainee.

This example may be seen to be well removed from the problem of a confrontation that anyone might encounter today or tomorrow, but the underlying message is the same. If you do not train or strive for some kind of realism and are never placed under pressure you will never quite be sure of how you will react.

Geoff Thompson is following in the footsteps of W.E. Fairbairn and 'Bill' Sykes and is to be lauded for that. He brings truth and common sense back into the gamut of 'self-defence' training, where nonsense and ignorance had reigned. Like Fairbairn and Sykes he has the courage and spirit of a warrior, but more importantly like Fairbairn and Sykes he has the compassion and control of a gentleman.

More than ever in the martial arts today, we must be seen as *sleeping tigers* and not as *rabid dogs*, bearing in mind that the sleeping tiger should not be of the paper type.

Read on, enjoy and like myself be amazed and educated by what this book contains.

Introduction

Firstly, thank you very much for taking the time to read this book, I hope that you find something within that will be of help in preparing you, your students and your art for an arena that is as savage as it is unrelenting.

As with all my books this is based on my own empirical study: with many hundreds of street fights under my belt I feel ideally positioned to help those that seek help (and apparently get on the tits of those that think they do not need help). I don't want to sound like a poser when I talk about *how many fights I've been involved in*, but if you've bought this book then I'm sure that you want to know where I'm coming from. I don't want you to think that I'm yet another *dry land swimmer* preaching about how it feels to get *wet*, neither do I want to sound patronising. I am extremely conscientious about my teaching and writing and will not write what I think people want to hear simply to sell a book, what I will write though is how it is. If my honesty offends please accept my apologies before we begin. I'm not here to offend anyone, that's not my game. I love all the arts and have studied most, but if you want to make them work for you a dose of self-honesty is an imperative; open your ears and take a hard look at the art you are learning, indeed teaching. Many people ask me to show them *truth* and then close their eyes to my demonstrations because it is not what they want to see, others ask me to tell them the *truth* and then close their ears to my words because, again, it is not what they want to hear.

Please do not be one of those people. Truth is often harder than a big bag of hard things, but honesty is the only way, so be honest with yourself, strip the bullshit from the art that you are studying and ask yourself, *is this really going to work for me outside the chip-shop?* If the answer is negative or even vague start trying to find ways to *make* it work or change it for one that will work. Without any shadow of a doubt this book will help you in that quest.

It would seem that in delivering what I would classify as educational books and articles I have ruffled one or two feathers. It would also seem that some are *shocked*, no less, by what I have to say. They think that I'm a thug. To these people I would say: *Shocked?* Let me tell you my good and sensitive people that if you are so easily shocked within the pages of a text, methinks that you tigers must be of the paper variety. I dread to think how shocked you will be then when society's grotesque minority shatter your porcelain lives with their *shocking* tactics and leave you in a bloodied heap because you failed to heed the warnings and worse still failed to pass on the tidings to your students and loved ones.

Shock is not a word in a sentence; it's a broken glass in the eye. *Shock* is not a sentence in a paragraph, it's three fuck-ugly youths with a punch-up-penchant who take your baby out of its pram and say: 'Give me your purse or the kid goes in the canal'. Neither is shock a paragraph on a page, a page in a book or even a book in a collection. No! Shock is being so frightened by the bastards that threaten you that you can't sleep nights, it's the two a.m. voice on the phone that says: 'I'm going to kill your wife and your children', real shock is a face full of ignited petrol because you dared to tackle a burglar in your own home and finally, oh ye of the sensitive heart, shock is the judicial system that feeds the predator and starves the victim. So when we are talking about *shocking*, please, let's keep things in context.

Apologies if I seem a little overzealous but we are not living in an idyllic world where my base tactics would be unnecessary, we are living in a violent society where they often are. I have used all of the tactics that I endorse to protect myself and to protect others though I always without exception recommend *flight above fight*. If flight is negated we are left with a choice, be the hammer or the anvil. No one can make that choice for you but be warned that the consequences of coming second on the pavement arena can mean anything from a punch in the eye to a hole in the ground; which is your attacker's choice, not yours.

Many people feel, as a for instance, that biting is a gratuitous act and hey - don't let the kids see that whatever you do. Do me a favour: check out the Kata you teach your children in every training session, finger strikes that would crush the windpipe and kill, single finger strikes that would blind even with minimum force, ankle stamps that are so potent they were taught in the second world war as killing blows, head butts? Do you teach your kids that or wouldn't that be classed as *karate*? They're in your Kata too, Harry Cook was in Japan when Yahara sensie scored an ippon (full point) in the J.K.A. championships with a head butt that echoed all around the contest arena . . . I don't remember anyone calling him a thug. In Kata there are also leg breaks, back breaks, wrist breaks etc. Are we thugs because we practice Kata? In many of the ancient Kung-fu systems students practiced jaw exercises to aid biting technique: are these masters thugs? I think not.

Martial art by definition means designed for war. What is war? The greatest expression of violence known to man. In war we brutally kill our fellow human beings, we torture them, blow them apart, sometimes in hundreds, thousands, even millions, then we congratulate ourselves on a job well done. Well done and legalised in the name of religion, politics, survival: put any name you like to it, no matter, someone will sanction it, especially if there is money involved. Now my friends, that's what I call shocking.

I am also told by the uninitiated that what I teach is 'not karate', and some of these people hold grades as high as fourth and fifth Dan. How did you all manage to get to such a high grade without knowing your bunkai? I teach boxing, wrestling, choking, butting, biting, stamping, awareness (zanshin), line-ups, distance control, deception etc and my learned friends say *that's not Karate*. Really? Have a close look at the system you're in and tell me that all those elements and more are not there. Of course they are there, they're just not taught on the curriculum.

To deal with a gratuitous enemy we need to employ gratuitous tactics, anything less and you'll be laughed off the planet . . . and then battered. If a finger in the eye is what is needed to stop an attacker or a bite or an incidental weapon, use it. It is a ridiculous concept to restrict yourself morally, or your students, by disallowing certain techniques against an enemy who will use everything and anything in his bid to damage. Only a fool would go to a gunfight with a feather duster.

First and foremost I teach humility and respect. I have a whole gamut of avoidance techniques that I employ before even thinking about a physical response, everything from avoidance to escape to loop-holing, verbal dissuasion, posturing – the list goes on. I believe that the vast majority of physical encounters can be avoided if you use awareness and leave you ego in the other suit. But if a situation becomes physical I do not limit myself or those I teach to socially palatable techniques, if I did that I wouldn't be able to teach them anything because all the techniques that really work are obese in their ugliness. Any kind of physical response is a lower echelon choice, but if it is survival that we are talking about then this may be your only choice. And if you get into a fight for any other reason than survival then I'd say that you made the wrong choice.

There are so many great things that I want to do with my life, so many great things, and punching some brain-shy on the nose because he looked at my pint is not one of them. I never want to get into a fight ever again in this incarnation, but I am not naive enough to believe that it might not happen, and when it does I need to know that my technique and character will not crumble under the weight of a real fight. That's what Animal Day is all about, it'll prepare you the chip-shop-debacle.

The interesting thing is that when you learn to do it for the real, to the point that you have no doubts about your art or your character, you will find – like me –that you no longer want to do it, you'll have so much respect for your ability and skills that you will not want to use them on others unless your choice car is empty. Your new found skill will enable you to walk away with confidence.

Respectfully, try not to look for the things that I do wrong, if you do you will fail to see the things that I'm doing right.

Note:
As with all of my books there are inevitable interlinks, I may intentionally or inadvertently quote from my other books, often using whole chapters if a point needs illustrating. So if I do repeat myself and you've heard some of it before please bear with me. I have to class each book as if it were the only one you have read, just in case it is. For instance I cannot leave out the section on the

inner opponent because it's in the *Fear* book - you may not have read the *Fear* book. Having said that I don't think it hurts to re-read the kind of information herein.

Chapter One

Why Pressure Test?

If you worked in a factory making manifolds for cars you wouldn't see a single manifold leave the factory gates without first being pressure tested, because the reliability of the car is determined by that manifold (or any other part). If the manifold does not stand up to the pressure test it does not leave the factory. We work in a factory called a dojo or gym, we give our students metaphoric manifolds called technique and character, then we send them out on to the violent streets without pressure testing either; then we wonder *what went wrong* when they collapse under the pressure of a real situation.

Would you ride a roller coaster that hadn't been safety tested? Would you travel in an aeroplane without a pressure tested engine or go down in a submarine that has not been *water-proofed*? No? Neither would I.

Training in the martial arts is a little like immersing a bicycle inner tube into a bowl of water, and then applying air pressure to find out where the leaks are. Rising bubbles indicate leakage, so we take the tube out of the water, get out the puncture kit and fix it.

The last thing you want as a martial art practitioner is to find that your technique or character crumbles in a confrontational situation.

Animal Day

It could get you killed or certainly badly injured. The controlled environment is the place to find the leaks, not the live scenario. By applying artificial pressure in a controlled environment one can find the bubbles and then fix the leaks without fear of being badly maimed or killed.

Therefore this book is all about exploring different ways in which we can supply that artificial pressure so that when confronted by an adverse situation in the street we will already know how well our technique and character will stand up to *pressure*.

The *live* scenario is about understanding the enemy and understanding the self (to steal a line from my late friend Sun Tzu). Understanding the enemy is knowing his game plan, his ritual of attack and his strengths, weaknesses, lair, the deception that he will employ as a precursor to attack, his mental and physical armour chinks, how he is likely to react to different stimuli like aggression, passivity, pain, fear, power etc, understanding that the enemy is unlikely to wear a stocking mask and hold a swag bag and cosh and demand 'give us your cash you beggar or I'll swipe you with me cosh'. Rather he will probably seem a rather ordinary person/s asking for the time or directions who suddenly transforms into an ugly attacking demon that shocks you so rigid that you are unable to activate a positive response.

We must also understand that a good street fighter will probably tell you that he does not want to fight before he takes you off the planet with a practiced right and a base fighter will probably drop into single syllables like 'Yeah!', 'And!', or 'So!' and go through a ritual of body language as a precursor to attack.

The art that many of us practice was designed to fight an antiquated enemy; the enemy of today is different. In fact the contemporary aggressor is very different from that of even a decade ago and of two decades ago. We are dealing with a foe that is likely to change with each subsequent generation. Therefore we must adapt our art and tailor it to the present; anything else belongs in the antiques store. I could go on all day about the traits of the enemy but that would be out of the context of this book, so for more about understanding the enemy see my book *Dead or Alive*.

Understanding yourself is what this book is all about. How will you react when the shit hits the fan? Will your technique work for you when you're so scared that all you want is your mother? In fact have you ever felt like that. I have, and on many occasions, that's why I know the importance of developing a will that is able to over ride this strong emotion. Will it work when blood is gushing from your smashed teeth, broken nose, smashed knee cap, broken wrist, or when you're exhausted or nauseous, when you're outnumbered, outweighed or simply out of your depth? Will your character stand up to the threat of aftermath, *comebacks*, threatening phone calls, police involvement, and intimidation?

At the end of the day do you really want to wait until it happens to find out. Wouldn't you rather measure your own response to stress in a controlled environment so that you can learn to understand your own body and therefore fix up all the leaky bits so that you are better prepared?

Pressure testing may differ from one person to another. What I find demanding you may feel very comfortable with and vice-versa, often you may have a good understanding of what puts you under pressure, other times you will not know and will only find out when exposed to different kinds of stressful stimuli.

Adversity, must therefore be sought and confronted so as to highlight weakness in technique and/or character and then confronted again and again to gain familiarity and desensitisation. This is, of course, hands on stuff and cannot be confronted through the pages of a book or through the chalk of a demonstration blackboard.

Animal Day is a term that I coined many years ago and is, basically a universal way of pressure testing technique and character in the controlled environment, but let's not pretend, there will be elements missing that can only be found in a *live* scenario. What *Animal Day* will do though is get you as close as damn it.

Sugar Ray Leonard once said to my friend, European pro Boxing champ Jim McDonnell, that boxing at a high level is 90% mental. Coping with a real fight is exactly the same, the physical part is the easy bit, it is the mental part that really hurts. Coping with *think-fight*, *pre-fight* and *post-fight* is a lot harder than coping with *in-fight*. *In-fight* is very tangible, it can be dealt with, often instinctively, it will look after itself, if your training is good you will cope with *in-fight* well, if your training is unrealistic then you will fall.

What we will try to discover in this text is your own personal limitations and then help to expand your limitations. So consider this book as a home pressure test kit and puncture outfit.

Chapter Two

Understanding Yourself

Understanding yourself is a complex matter. Some go through a whole lifetime without discovering even the fundamentals. By stepping into adversity (whatever your adversity might be) you will find out in a hurry exactly who you are and what your limitations are. In Latin they call it *per ardua et astra*, which means 'through hardship to the stars'. The famous American Dog Brothers have a similar saying *higher consciousness through harder contact.* Don't be surprised when/if you find out that you are not quite the person you think you are when you look in the reality mirror. When I first looked, I have to say that initially I was a little disappointed, my limitations were greater than I had imagined in my mind's eye. Later I learned to take an altogether more philosophical view of my 'rising bubbles', rather than feeling disappointed I felt excited that I had located my stress fractures and was now able to mend them and make myself a stronger and more complete martial artist. The interesting thing was that once I had sealed my major leaks my confidence blossomed and I no longer felt the need to get into street fights just to prove my ability, in fact quite the opposite was true, with my new found confidence I developed the ability to walk away from confrontation, to let the other fellow off as it were. My own students and instructors feel the same way, pressure testing has made them very gentle people, and subsequently what they teach beyond Animal Day is the art of gentleness, the art of letting people off.

Animal Day

Most don't realise their own weaknesses until it is too late, they lie in bed (maybe a hospital bed), after handling a confrontational situation badly, and think to themselves *what went wrong?* Understanding yourself means recognising your own personal weaknesses and strengths and also understanding that you can and will lose if you are not absolutely *on the ball*. It also means understanding the strengths and weaknesses of the system that you are practicing. Former and latter require honesty in bag-fulls.

One associate on a training course told me that he asked his martial arts master what he should do when a fight hit the floor (goes to ground work), his master said, 'We don't fight on the floor'. Draw your own conclusions.

To understand the self, one must understand the bodily reactions that we all feel in confrontational situations, firstly lets look at the basics of fear (for a greater insight see my book *Fear – the friend of exceptional people*).

Fear:

What is fear? How can one define it? The English dictionary informs us that fear is:

An unpleasant, often strong emotion caused by anticipation or awareness of danger.

In layman's terms when the brain senses danger it triggers adrenalin, this being a human turbo charge, brought on by awareness/ anticipation to aid *fight or flight*. This unpleasant, often strong emotion causes terror immobilisation, or the freeze syndrome in the recipient. The key with adrenalin is, don't panic. Harness and utilise adrenalin, fine tune it into a laser beam of action that can be turned on and off with pin-point accuracy, missiled into your response with devastating explosiveness.

Adrenalin is a little like *fuel injection* or *turbo drive* in a sports car; action, the metaphoric accelerator.

The car: by engaging the clutch, and pressing the accelerator you will utilise the *turbo*, and the car will move at speed. However, if you sit at the traffic lights pressing your foot on the accelerator with out engaging the clutch, there will be no movement and the engine will be flooded, all the fuel will be wasted.

The human: by engaging *action* (fight/flight) you will utilise the *turbo drive* of adrenalin, and trigger spontaneous response.

However, if *action* is not engaged and panic sets in, energy will be wasted and you will be flooded and overwhelmed by this natural energy force.

Body accelerators

Positive body accelerator
Your positive body accelerator is *action*. When you act (engage the clutch), i.e. confront your fear, adrenalin is utilised positively, adding vigour to your response.

Negative body accelerator
Your negative body accelerator is *panic*, this is caused when the reasoning process mistakes adrenalin for fear. More adrenalin is then released and one is flooded with fuel, this leaves the recipient drained of energy and often frozen in the face of ensuing danger.

Animal Day

If you find yourself in a confrontational situation and do not or cannot *act*, the adrenalin will be perpetuated by increasing panic. Like the car, you will be pressing the accelerator with out engaging the clutch. Nothing is gained and all is lost.

In the gap between confrontation and action, adrenalin can be controlled with deep breathing and knowledge, and the look of fear hidden with *the duck syndrome* .

Through my own search and experimentation I have learned that the explosion inside the stomach that so many people struggle with and that causes the infamous *freeze* syndrome, is adrenalin. In primeval days when mankind had to fight to live and eat, the feeling of fear was an every day occurrence that would have felt as natural and as common as eating or drinking. In today's society, which is very tame by comparison, adrenalin is no longer needed in our everyday lives, in fact some people go through a whole lifetime without ever experiencing it fully, so when a situation arises that causes the adrenalin to flow, and because we are so unfamiliar with it (unlike our pre-historic ancestors) we, naturally, neither welcome, use nor like it.

We panic.

Psychologists call it the *fight or flight* syndrome. In moments of danger/confrontation the body releases a hormonal messenger from the adrenals that hits and go through the bloodstream like a speeding train, preparing the body for *fight or flight*, deeming it stronger, faster and partially (sometimes completely) anaesthetized to pain.

• The more demanding the situation the bigger the build-up and adrenalin release.

• The bigger the release the better you perform (run, fight).

• But by the same count, the bigger the build-up and release, the harder it is to control.

Adrenalin is released in several ways: there is slow release, fast release, aftermath and *combo*. I will take them in turn.

Slow release (think-fight)
When you anticipate confrontation the body releases adrenalin slowly and often over a long period. The slow release is not so intense as the fast release but, due to its longevity, it can wear and corrode the recipient. Things like anticipation of having to talk in public, a big sales meeting, a forthcoming karate competition, a planned confrontation with the husband/wife/neighbour/boss etc. will cause slow release often up to months before the expected confrontation. Boxers often have to cope with think-fight for months before a fight.

Fast release (pre-fight fear)
Psychologists like to call this *adrenal dump*, the bodyguards list it as the WOW factor. The fast release occurs when anticipation is not present, or when a situation escalates unexpectedly fast, causing adrenal dump, this feeling is often so intense that the recipient freezes in the face of confrontation, the reasoning process mistaking it for sheer terror. This the most devastating of the three. Fast release occurs when a confrontation arises that one was not ready or prepared for, usually the same as those that cause slow release but without the prior notice. You are in a big meeting and

unexpectedly you are asked to address those present without any preparation or you are confronted, again without warning by your boss/neighbour/partner or an attacker etc.

In-fight release
Once a situation occurs the feeling of fear usually subsides, but if you struggle during the situation/fight and start to get the wrong end of a bad situation the body will, again, release adrenalin causing *freeze* or capitulation. The thought of losing, added to in-fight adrenalin, can cause terrible anxiety. It is a sign of strong character if you can override these feelings.

Aftermath
After confrontation, whether successful or not, the body often secretes slow releases of adrenalin, this being brought on possibly by the stress of *scenario overload*, when confrontation is so traumatic that is forces the body/mind into overload to cope leaving the recipient mentally and physically weak, and so vulnerable. It is also brought on by post confrontation anticipation, when the brain senses/dreads another confrontation or a repeat of the earlier confrontation it, again, releases adrenalin to prepare the body. Aftermath has been responsible for many sleepless nights.

Pre/post-fight trauma
From my experience many people bottle out before a fight due to pre/post-fight trauma. That is, worrying about the consequences of aftermath before the fight even begins. This is usually catalysed by the inner opponent who badgers you with the negative possibilities of your actions. This is especially so with a reputable fighter who has a name for *comebacks* (revenge attacks). Often you may know in your heart that you can beat the person but cannot handle the thought of aftermath, ie. come-backs, police

involvement, badly injuring your opponent or being badly injured yourself. Part of dealing with this is, as Sun Tzu says *counting the cost before engaging in battle*. You must look at all the possible consequences of your actions and accept responsibility for them before you engage in battle. You must tell yourself that *whatever happens, I'll handle it* (greater detail in the *Fear* book).

Adrenal Combo
Those working/living in a stress related environment, the stock exchange, business, security etc. may experience a combination (combo) of the latter. Slow release because they anticipate confrontation, adrenal dump when situations unexpectedly occur in their environment and aftermath, in relation to situations that have already happened. At once the recipient may experience a concoction of all four.

All of the pre-described feelings are as natural as the feelings of hunger and thirst, also they are all controllable. The important thing initially is accepting the fact that they are natural and that you are not different or a coward because you have these feelings. When there is confrontation of any kind there will be adrenalin, it will never go away, though you will learn to control and harness those feelings.

The duck syndrome
In many aspects of confrontation, certainly business and combat, it can be to the recipient's detriment to show that he is suffering the ills of fear, this often being seen as a weak link, so it is profitable to be able to hide the physical manifestations of adrenalin. Even in nature, a dog will attack when he senses fear, the same can be said in all walks of life.

Animal Day

A duck will appear to glide through the water with grace and elegance. Under the water his little webbed feet will be going like the clappers. When you understand and can control the adrenal flow it is possible to hide adrenal reaction ('going like the clappers') by appearing unmoved and calm. This deceives those around you into believing that you are not scared. As an old sage once said, 'When ignorance is mutual, confidence is king.' (For detail on how to use *adrenalin switches* to beat your opponent see *Dead or Alive*).

As I mentioned before, recognising the feeling of fear and understanding its mechanics will help to minimize its shock impetus.

These are the natural bodily reactions to adrenalin:

Pre fight shakes
Your legs, and possibly other limbs, may shake uncontrollably.

Dry mouth
Your mouth may become dry and pasty.

Voice quiver
Your voice may acquire a nervous and audible tremor.

Tunnel vision
On the positive side, tunnel vision enhances visual concentration. Its negative by-product is blinkering of peripheral vision.

Sweaty palms and forehead
The palms of the hands and forehead often sweat profusely.

Nausea
Adrenalin may cause vomiting, or the feeling of vomiting.

Bowel loosening
The recipient may experience constant urges to use the toilet.

'Yellow' fever
Adrenalin, certainly adrenal dump, evokes feelings of helplessness and abject terror. Fear of confrontation may bring on an extreme feeling of depression and foreboding. Tears may also occur.

Time distortion
Many reported that confrontation seemed to last an eternity, when in reality it may have only lasted a few minutes. During confrontation time can appear to stand still, one minute often feeling like one hour. Paradoxically, in retrospect, many have said, 'It all happened so fast'. When interviewing James, the victim of an unsolicited assault, he initially told me that he was attacked without warning. After talking to him at some length it turned out that, between first seeing his attackers and the attack itself, there was a time lapse of 11 seconds, this being lost to time distortion.

Restless nights
Many suffer from restless nights when experiencing slow release and aftermath.

Irritability
Constant exposure often makes the recipient irritable and bad tempered, this is often as much caused by lack of food and sleep as anything else.

No appetite
Appetite tends to lessen, often resulting in weight loss, especially with slow release and aftermath.

Poor sex drive
Appetite for sex can be seriously curbed.

Increased heart rate
Due to the turbo drive of adrenalin the heart rate often increases to what the recipient may feel is an abnormal rate, some may even experience chest pains as a result of tenseness in the pectoral region.

Depression
As a result of all the inner turmoil brought on by anticipation, depression often occurs.

These are not the only bodily reactions to adrenalin, though they are certainly the main ones. Other reactions may occur as a direct result of confrontation.

All of the forgoing feelings are usual, accept and ignore them, they are all part and parcel of adrenal reaction and, though unpleasant, quite natural. The feelings cannot hurt or harm you and they do lessen in intensity as you become more exposed to them.

Now let's have a look at some of the things that can force capitulation in a real fight, and often in the controlled arena also.

1) Aggression

Many people are psyched out in real situations by aggression, as soon as the attacker becomes aggressive they capitulate, this is also true in the controlled arena. The simple truth is *raw aggression scares people.* I have beaten many opponents in the street with aggression alone, this is because aggression registers *danger* with the subconscious mind, even when, in the controlled area, the conscious mind knows that there is no danger, the subconscious still reacts to aggression by switching on adrenalin to aid response, the reasoning process mistakes adrenalin for fear and hey presto the recipient is scared.

2) Non-Aggression

Often when a situation is occurring the opponent or potential attacker may be completely non-aggressive, in theory this shouldn't scare us but in reality it often does because we equate non-aggression for non-fear. The sub-conscious mind believes, some times rightly, that the non-aggressive predator is emotionless and feels no fear, this unnerves the mind and again intimates danger causing adrenal flow. Non-aggression is usually a sign that the aggressor is over confident or very experienced in the duck syndrome.

2) Contact

Whether the contact be poking, grabbing, pulling or attacking, in or out of the controlled arena physical contact psyches people out and for the same reason as aggression, the subconscious mind anticipates danger and switches the adrenalin on, again causing the recipient to feel fear.

I have demonstrated this in the controlled arena, firstly telling a volunteer that no matter what I do or say he will be in no danger, then I pretend to get aggressive and poke him in the chest. I tell him that I am going to knock him out. Even though, on a conscious level he knows that he is in absolutely no danger his subconscious mind, working completely independently senses danger and activates *fight or flight*.

3) Eye Contact

Have you ever been in a pub or a restaurant and someone has stared at you menacingly across the room and you've instantly felt scared? I have. The visual stimuli of silent aggression sends the message to the brain that there might be danger, the brain activates adrenalin, the recipient feels fear.

Size

The physical size of an opponent often causes the brain to over exaggerate the situation believing that size is synonymous with strength/ability when of course it is not, never the less the brain activates adrenalin to help you out, just in case. Paradoxically you may be faced with an opponent who is small/light, the fact that he is there and ready to fight intimates to the sub-conscious mind that there is more danger than is outwardly apparent, after all if he is that small and still wants to fight me *he must be good*. This is especially so if the little opponent is very aggressive or overly cool.

Reputation

The brain often activates *adrenal dump* when faced with a reputable fighter, sensing extreme danger. This happens in the controlled arena and on the pavement arena. Adrenal dump is the hardest form of adrenalin to control because it comes so fast and without warning. The recipient feeling, mistakenly, immediate fear, this leaving the door wide open for the inner opponent who goes to work on the inner destruction that leaves you beaten even before raising a guard. It is very hard for the eyes to see what the mind has got completely out of focus. With a reputable fighter you will be thinking of everything at once and capitulation often occurs.

4) Tiredness

When the body gets tired during confrontation, the subconscious mind, realising that tiredness can lead to defeat, injects the recipient with the turbo drive of adrenalin in a bid to salvage a bad situation. Again the recipient panics, thinking it's fear, the panic uses up the adrenalin negatively and often causes capitulation.

Pain/Injury

Pain, caused by injury is the body's way of saying *stop*, any more may be detrimental. Our innate survival instincts, again on a subconscious level, are often set at a very low tolerance rate causing us to abort long before we reach our desired goals, these *cut-out* points have to be extended to allow greater tolerance, in some cases even erased completely. Pain is the biggest stopping point for most people. Also pain/injury will register with the brain as danger and activate adrenalin which will act as an anesthetic, whilst it does do this it also causes the fear syndrome. So where adrenalin should offer fight/flight/anesthesia to aid survival it causes *freeze* which often begets defeat.

Nausea

If you reach nausea it can mean one of several things; if you reach it very quickly it may be because you are unfit, if you are you will feel sick very quickly, or it may be a reaction to adrenalin (a by-product of adrenalin can be nausea). You may be fit but have still, due to an elongated battle, reached your physical limitations. This feeling can also cause adrenalin because the subconscious senses that there is a danger of defeat.

The Inner Opponent

At the base of all the aforementioned (and you may well add more to the list) is the inner opponent.

Animal Day

This from my book *Fear - the friend of exceptional people*:

The ugly hand maiden of fear is the omniscient Mr Negative, General Sun Tzu called him the inner opponent, Susan Jeffers, in her book *Feel the fear - and do it anyway*, called him the chatterbox, I call him Mr Negative. That negative voice that perches on the shoulder of your minds eyes and tells you that you're frightened, scared or that you *can't handle it* (the situation). Many people are not beaten by their fear, rather they are beaten by their own minds. A negative notion that latches on to a subconscious insecurity soon grows into a monstrously big *inner opponent* that forces people to acquiesce a lot sooner that they should. The inner opponent is responsible for beating more people that any tangible or intangible fear. It is fair to say that if you cannot beat the man on the inside then you cannot beat the man on the outside.

I remember a wonderful story about a wrestler who was travelling by train from Glasgow to London to wrestle the legendary Bert Asarati, renowned for *hurting* his opponents. All the way down on the train journey the wrestler fought with his inner opponent who kept on reminding him of the prowess of Mr Asarati. Every time the train stopped at a station the wrestler's inner opponent tempted him to get off and go back to Glasgow, at each station the inner opponent getting stronger and stronger, the wrestlers will getting weaker and weaker. By Birmingham the wrestler could stand no more. He got off the train and caught the next back to Glasgow. Mr Asarati received a note from the wrestler that said, 'Gone back to Glasgow, you beat me in Birmingham'. His inner opponent defeated him hours before he was due to enter the ring.

This story will be familiar to many, only the opponent may not have been an 18 stone wrestler, rather a big business deal, the decision to change job/home/car/relationship, ask the boss for a rise, travel the world, start up a new business, expand an existing business. To the phobic it may have been leaving the house, going in a plane, travelling in a car, going in a lift, up an escalator etc. Many are beaten before the fight by their own minds. Why? Because it takes no effort to think negative thoughts, the inner opponent will do that for you, to think positive thoughts however takes a lot of effort.

This from James Clavel's book *Shogan*:

To think bad thoughts is really the easiest thing in the world. If you leave your mind to its self it will spiral you down into ever increasing unhappiness. To think good thoughts, however, requires effort. This is one of the things that training and discipline are about. So teach you mind to dwell on sweet perfumes, the touch of silk, tender rain drops against the shoji, the tranquillity of dawn, then at length you won't have to make such an effort and you will be of value to yourself.

Left to its own devices, the mind can be a self-detonating time bomb of negativity that will spiral you down into ever increasing misery. Dealing with the inner opponent is firstly about understanding that *everyone* has an inner opponent (often there is more than one voice), though very few come to terms with him, and also understanding that we will never reach our full potential whilst he has the run of our heads. Mr Negative is very controllable, if you know how.

These are three ways that I have found successful in dealing with Mr Negative:

1) Thought rejection

Reject the negative thoughts by completely ignoring them, not listening to anything that Mr Negative says, thus leaving him no mental ledge on which to perch.

This is harder than it seems and demands self-discipline. Negative thoughts have a habit of swimming into your mind, uninvited and at will. Don't have any of it. It is your mind, you are in charge. Occupy your mind by reading, listening to the radio, by keeping yourself busy, watching the box, anything to take your mind away from the negative thoughts. Don't give in and panic with the thoughts because that will cause them to multiply tenfold and then twenty fold, before you know it your mind has been overrun by negative emotion that can quickly turn to depression. So, just ignore them. In combat keep check on the negative thoughts by focusing on the situation at hand, if negative thoughts try to enter your head do not even acknowledge them.

2) Thought counter attack

If you can't come to terms with this try thought counter attack (this is the method that I practice). Fight your inner opponent by countering every *negative* thought he throws at you with a *positive* thought of your own.

Inner opponent	*You're scared.*
Your counter	*No, I'm not scared.*
Inner opponent	*You can't handle this situation.*
Your counter	*Yes, I can handle this situation, I can handle anything.*
Inner opponent	*You're out of your depth, you'll never cope.*
Your counter	*I'm not out of my depth and I can cope, in fact I'll cope easily.*
Inner opponent	*You'll fail and everyone will laugh.*
Your counter	*If that's the worse that can happen, I can handle it.*

3) Repetitive Mantra

Just keep repeating to yourself: 'I can handle it, I can handle it, I can handle it'. This allows no room for negative thoughts to infiltrate your mind.

By controlling your thoughts you will erase the negativity. You have to learn not to take any crap from the inner opponent and fight, tooth and nail, every time that he rears his ugly head. Watch out though, he can be a cheeky beggar, if you are not vigilant he will try to sneak in when you least expect. Even the feelings that accompany negativity can be countered with defiance. I always tell myself, 'Do your worst, I can handle it, I can handle twice what you're giving me'. The biggest fight is always with yourself and the more wins you get under your belt the stronger you become and the weaker your inner opponent becomes. Once you have the inner opponent under control you are well on the way.

Fight back negativity right from the onset. Each negative thought you allow to penetrate your psyche may, and usually does, erode a small part of your *will* until eventually you are defeated. I work on the premise that *negative begets negative begets defeat*. As a parallel, *positive begets positive, begets victory*.

Your greatest enemy in times of adversity is your own mind. Tell your inner opponent that you *can handle it*. Once you have come to terms with Mr. Negative and have learned to accept fear as a friend, allow adrenalin the run of your body, don't let yourself panic. Knowledge is power. By understanding your own body, by understanding the mechanics of adrenalin/fear you can learn self-control. Panic is catalysed by ignorance, by not understanding your own body, or its workings. Most people, in most situations are not defeated by their assailants, they are defeated by their own mind.

Animal Day

Adrenalin is a natural feeling that should be accepted with out panic. There is no way around these feelings, everyone feels them, they are a part and parcel of adversity.

Now let's look at the *excuse syndrome*. This is where the inner opponent will find you many seemingly legitimate excuses not to pressure test, you have to recognise these and be honest with yourself. Don't let silly excuses hinder your development. Whilst you might think that you will not get or use excuses to avoid the adversity of Animal Day you will get them and you will be tempted to use them, it is natural to feel these feelings, just don't go with them because if you're not getting wet then you're not learning to swim.

"If there is no adversity there is no advance."

The mind, or more specifically the inner opponent, will throw tangible or intangible excuses in your way to slow you down or stop you completely in your plight to pressure test.

The harder the confrontation becomes the more the excuses will flow. Look out for them, they will come.

If you really want to succeed nothing will stand in your way and no excuse will be good enough, if you are struggling any excuse will suddenly become a legitimate excuse.

By first recognising and then overcoming these excuses you will develop an indomitable spirit due to your overthrow of the inner opponent. Also gained will be enlightenment, because in order to get past the more difficult excuses it is necessary to dissect yourself mentally, admitting and recognising your weaknesses in order to be able to confront and overcome them, and thus get past whatever stumbling block it is that's holding you back.

The excuses that the inner opponent invents/finds are or can be many splendoured. They may be tangible or intangible. Basically speaking the excuses usually fall into three categories, though they are uniform in one element, they are all reasons to avoid adversity and pressure testing.

Recognising these excuses will help immeasurably in your bid to overcome them.

The three categories are: *Tangible*, *Intangible* and *Silly excuses*.

Tangible excuses

These are incidental excuses that are responsible for more bottle drops than any other. Broken bones, torn ligaments, twisted ankles, illnesses (even other people's illnesses), the list goes on.

Of course with a serious injury it is foolish to keep training as the injury/illness may be aggravated by your continuance. However, minor injuries should not deter you from conscientious practice.

You can quite easily train around such injuries. If your left hand is injured, train your right or vice versa. I was in and out of hospital, and plaster, for two years and had, in that time, two operations for a broken right wrist. I never missed training once and used the time to perfect my left hand techniques. I have also had broken bones all over my body, but still managed to train around my injuries. Training under such adverse conditions requires and develops real will-power and is a great character builder.

With the more serious injury/illness that does lay you off, the danger lies in whether or not you get back to training after your convalescence. From my experience, most people do not. While you are recovering try to visit your training establishment to maintain your ties and enthusiasm, this will greatly help in your re-start program when the obstacle of bad health is removed.

A lot of people use their injuries to opt out because they were finding the going getting tough anyway, but remember this, if it was easy everybody and his dog would be good.

Intangible excuses

These can be as destructive in your advancement as the tangibles and in a psychological sense far more painful. Also, because they are mental as opposed to physical, they can quite often be very difficult to admit or detect. The greatest intangible is *physical contact*, sparring or getting hit. A great percentage of people leave training because they are frightened of sparring. Even at the boxing club when I was coaching, it was common knowledge that you lost 85% of your new starters after you put them in the ring for the first time. The only way to overcome this is, firstly, to admit it. Don't be ashamed, everyone feels the same so you're not on your own. Secondly, confront it again and again until you become desensitized to it, and take heart, it does get better. The more you spar and put yourself in the firing line the better and more confident you will feel. In the world of real fighting, pain, unfortunately, is the ugly hand maiden, so it is imperative that you develop at least some tolerance for it if you want any chance of surviving a real situation.

Boredom

"It's getting boring." Boredom is another major excuse that loses many people from the martial arts arena and in my opinion, it is a lazy excuse. To develop a technique into an instinctive reflex, to develop power, speed, endurance, footwork, mental muscle or anything else worth having for that matter, requires repetition, and what is repetition if it isn't boring. Repetition is practised by the student revising for his doctorate, and paradoxically, by the soldier perfecting a bayonet attack. Swimmers will practice hours and hours a day perfecting a stroke and jugglers will juggle until their hands bleed, all in pursuit of excellence. As martial artists, we are no different. For one technique to be effective in a *live* situation we must do a thousand in the gym.

Boredom is the lazy man's excuse not to train. You treat boredom as another challenge that must be bettered if advancement is to be attained. When boredom sets in you must use concentration to push it back out again. Sheer concentration on the technique you are practising will erode boredom. You must practice a technique until you are sick to death of it, then you will get good at it. I have also found that people use the excuse of boredom when the going is getting a little too tough for them. *Oh I'm getting bored with this* can usually be translated as *I can't handle it*.

It is surprising, but true, that when people start training they will let nothing get in their way, nothing keeps them from their training, it's the most important thing in their lives, etc. Then when things get a little demanding every thing gets in their way, all of a sudden your training times collide with something else, or the wife's moaning, I've got to do overtime, take the dog to the vet, go to a funeral. Hey, believe me I know I made up all the same excuses before I got honest with myself. Don't take any bullshit from the inner opponent.

Animal Day

Lack of enjoyment

Lack of enjoyment in training is a brother to boredom. Another feeble excuse. Enjoyment in training comes and goes, nobody enjoys it all of the time. And certainly when you pressure test enjoyment goes right out of the window. The real enjoyment comes from the fruits of training rather than the actual training itself. After all, to become proficient we must push ourselves through the pain of a gruelling training session, who in their right mind enjoys pain, (my profuse apologies to all you masochists out there!). If you are going through a bad patch of not enjoying your training, stick with it and try to treat the training as a mundane task that has to be done, the enjoyment will return. It's unrealistic to expect enjoyment all the time out of something so physically and mentally demanding, when the enjoyment is there make the best of it, when it isn't, cope. It's all part of the character building process.

As with boredom this is usually another excuse to cover fear. Don't fall for it.

Lack of Improvement/success

Another favourite excuse for throwing in the towel is, *I don't seem to be getting any better.* This is one of the mind's best finishers and kills off many students with the suddenness of cyanide tea, after all, what is the point of continuing in training if you're not getting any better? If I may use a metaphor, it is a propelling spiral that picks up momentum very quickly, and just as it seems to be reaching its pinnacle of speed, it starts, or at least it would appear to be, going backwards. So it is with the martial arts, in the beginning you are learning something new every session and improvement can be as fast as the aforementioned metaphoric spiral. All of a sudden your advancement seems to be slowing down and in some cases you seem, (like the spiral), to be going backward instead of forward, but it is only an illusion. After such a quick advance even a slight decrease in speed may seem like a backward spiral, usually it is only the person himself who sees or thinks he sees this supposed decline, everyone around him will be seeing his improvement but him.

From my experience and as irony would have it, it is usually the better student who thinks he isn't improving. Every day and every session that you train will bring you, visible or invisible, large or small, some advancement. The child that you see everyday will show no visible change or growth, to the person who only sees the same child every few months, the change is so obvious that they sometimes can't believe it's the same child. And so it is with improvement in training, sometimes it is so gradual that on a day to day basis it is almost unnoticeable, but it will be there.

Silly Excuses

These are the most infuriating and are always employed by people who are using the *silly excuse* to cover a deeper, more underlying reason or problem, probably one of those in the last category. These are the worst, (and sometimes the funniest) reasons for missing single sessions or even packing in all together, because it means that the person employing the *silly excuse* cannot come to terms with the real reason.

To my mind this puts him right at the bottom of the proverbial mountain with a long way to go. He'll probably never make it unless he gets some real self honesty very quickly.

At the risk of repeating myself a bigger part of being able to confront is being able to understand. It is very hard to destroy what you cannot create. Hopefully this chapter and indeed this book will help you to understand your own body so that you are better able to deal with its reactions to conflict.

Chapter Three

Understanding Your Art

This is a sensitive area. So many people think that they have the complete art and that no one else has. They believe they are open-minded and others are not and that they have all the answers where others have only questions. Even the so called *new wave* martial artists who left tradition because of blinkered senior instructors and *the classical mess*, now wear their own blinkers like a thorny crown and have, in a way, created their own classical mess.

Every system has something to offer, and to say that they do not is to be blinkered. To trash all traditionalists simply because they are traditional, or to trash other stylists because they do not follow the same way as us would also be very blinkered. The one thing that all martial arts have in common is that they all have something to offer if we would only open our eyes wide enough to see.

Understanding your own art means little more than being honest, even if it is only with yourself.

Is your art a kicking art, punching art, or a grappling art? Is it close range, long range, semi-contact, full contact, an attacking art or a defensive art? Whatever your art is analyse what it is not, that will be where your weakness lies. It is also wise to place your main range under pressure just to make sure that you are as good at it (or it is as good) as you think.

It is also important to analyse whether your main range, be it kicking, punching or grappling is pre-dominantly short range or long range.

Are you a long-range kicker or a short-range kicker? Long range puncher or short range puncher. Whatever you are, again your weakness will lie in the range - within your main range - that you are weakest at. Then what you have to ask yourself is *am I effective at my main range?* Of course everyone likes to think that they are, but often they are not. This over-confidence often comes from being the big fish in a little pond. Take a step out of your comfort zone, step into a bigger pool and see just how good you are. Over-confidence is a killer, getting into the big pool and feeling completely out of your depth can be very scary, but quite liberating. I always place myself in a class where I know I am at the bottom, and then climb to the top, once I am at the top I move on to another class where I am at the bottom again. If, whilst you are reading this, you feel that you are already at the top then I can tell without even meeting you that you're not, just the fact that you think you are automatically disqualifies you from being so. Get down off that sugar pedestal. Look a little harder and you'll find some one to push you.

As an example, I would class you as a good puncher if you could do three rounds with a good boxer, I would consider you a good kicker if you could do three with a good Thai boxer and I would certainly consider you good in close if you could go five minutes with a good wrestler or Judoka.

As a young Karataka I was pre-dominantly a kicker, but thought myself a good puncher too. I'd worked on the weights all my life and had played with grappling so thought my ground work was competent. When I tried to place my limited skills in the real world of fighting I quickly realised that my main range, kicking, was immediately neutralised by my environment. Most fights start at conversation range, this being punching range, so there was no room to kick in most situations, if there was room it was quickly gobbled up by a greedy aggressor who wanted to be *in my face*. I was a strong puncher, I could hit the bag hard, but basically I was a long range, straight puncher and conditioned to pull my blows on impact.

Real fighting is very close range and often demands the better suited hook or uppercut, but they weren't on my curriculum. The first time I hit someone I automatically pulled the punch on impact, I also felt out of range, a range that seemed to disappear before my eyes and wouldn't stay still for a second. The first time I went to grappling in the street I didn't have a clue what to do, I bludgeoned my way through and made a hard and long job out of some thing that should have been clinical. I was also completely unaccustomed to raw aggression and didn't know how to react to verbal. People were throwing verbal attacks and I didn't know how to defend, counter attack or even simply attack. Most of what goes in a real fight is not in the physical it's psychological. Openers, weakeners, primers and even finishing blows are secured with dialogue, the attacker using verbal missiles to attack the psyche. All I knew, all my art had taught me, was the physical response, a little like teaching someone how to dive in the swimming pool but not teaching him how to swim.

It is true that fighting arts teach you distancing and timing etc, but the distancing in the street is different from that of the dojo and so is the timing because the fighting is so frantic and staccato, it is also different because it's enforced by the enemy and the environment.

So be realistic when evaluating your art: if you think that your art is good, test it. Not just at strongest end but also at the weakest end, where the leaks are, then set about sealing up those leaks. As they say, *a chain is only as strong as its weakest link*. If you are a crap grappler, or a crap puncher then you are only as strong as that weakness (crap!) because the first time it goes to that range might be the very first time you get into a fight.

One of the main weaknesses that I have found in the arts that I have studied, and I have studied most of them, is that they all, with the exception of western boxing, condition their practitioners to fight defensively, certainly when they teach the self-defense aspect of the art. They teach their practitioners to wait for the attacker to attack, then block and counter attack. In the real world? TOO LATE! Too late by a long shot. It doesn't take much logic to realise that action is quicker than reaction.

If you let someone attack you first and expect to block and counter think again. In the dojo, when the distance and conditions are perfect and when you know what the attacker is going to attack with and when and how and with how much intensity, sure then it will work. Outside, from eighteen inches, with no prior knowledge of which attack and when or even why; not quite so likely.

It is my opinion, after spending a decade working with violence, that a defensive art in a live situation is about as useful as a cat flap in an elephant house. I'm not saying that it won't work in ideal circumstances on the odd occasion or for the 9's and 10's (on a skill scale of 1-10, 9's and 10's are the cream of the crop, 2's and 3's the average practitioner) but in normal circumstances and for the average-good practitioner, very unlikely. In a real situation if you are not attacking you'll be getting attacked. If you are facing more than one opponent, and waiting to defend, you are in even more trouble because multiple attackers do not stand in line waiting their turn to attack, they strike as one. If you think that blocking one person is hard try blocking two or three or four . . . at the same time. There may be a system out there that can do what I am saying cannot be done, if there is I have never seen it.

In *Animal Day*, you may test your system to the full where you will be working with uncompliant opponents who will be unsympathetic to weakness in spirit or technique. If you hold your kick out too long or pivot on one leg after retracting the kick you will be grabbed and grappled. If your punches lack power or accuracy or if you over commit or under-commit, they will be crushed without mercy. If you are a grappler with no knowledge of punching, kicking or atemi jutsu (striking whilst grappling) you will pick up major injuries as you close distance or inside grappling range. In Animal Day you will see little or no trapping, the distance is only there for a fleeting second before it is swallowed up by flailing/colliding bodies.

If compliancy reigns, and it seems to in many of the systems around today, everything will work, it will also be very impressive. A wrist lock is excruciating if you allow someone to place it on you, because of the pain you may think, *yeah, that's brilliant, really effective*. Don't forget though, it is only effective because you allowed it to be put on. The time when a technique is effective is when it is put on against your will. Of course it is good to practice, to a degree, with compliancy, that's how you learn and perfect technique, but at some stage you will have to practice against mass uncompliancy to see if it will really work. Everything changes when a situation becomes *live*. Distances change, attitudes change, timing changes, stamina, will, pain tolerance . . . it all changes. I was talking to Jim McDonnell (European pro boxing champion) yesterday about this exact thing and he told me about the time he and one of his stable mates met to fight for a vacant title (this story is told by Jim in *Fear - the friend of exceptional people*). Now in the gym and on paper the two fighters were absolutely equal on all counts and when they sparred in the gym there was nothing in it. Every one said what a cracking fight it was going to be, all expecting it to go the full distance. When the fight actually took place Jim stopped his man in the first round. Jim puts this down to the fact that he could perform the same at show time as he could in the relatively safe environs of the practice gym, his opponent could not. He could do it in the gym all day long but add pressure to the scenario and he fell apart.

Bob Spour, my friend and top Thai man told me of the time he was teaching one of his senior students knife fighting, the fighting was very close range, fast and skilful. When they stopped for a breather Bob exchanged the dummy practice knifes for live blades and said, 'O.K. let's try with real knives now'. Suddenly the distance changed, what was very short range suddenly became very long range and what was fast, skilful and flowing became slow, stuttered and amateur. The introduction of pressure puts every thing into true perspective. That's what Animal Day will do for you, give you a true perspective of REAL, so forget all this bollocks about *we daren't practice full out because our art is too dangerous,* try it full out and see just how dangerous it is, I guarantee that it will not be so dangerous as you think it will be.

One of the Gracie's opponents when accepting a challenge with one of the Gracie's students said, 'Perhaps I should wear gloves, I don't want to hurt my opponent too much.' Gracie replied, 'Try and hurt him as much as you can.' Within seconds of the fight beginning the Gracie student took his opponent to the floor, without even receiving a blow, and finished the fight with a choke.

The acid test of *real* is pressure. No pressure no guarantee.

Animal Day

So have a good look at your own art and see where the weaknesses lie, if you're not sure try Animal Day to find out. When you have found out work and improve the strengths and weaknesses. No one style has all the answers so you may have to beg, steal and borrow from other systems or perhaps dig a little deeper into your own system for some hidden bunkai (applications hidden in Kata and forms) but more than anything else . . . be honest with yourself.

Here is a little run down on what I find effective/ineffective about different systems.

Karate

Taking into consideration the different style etc, Karate is at its best whilst in kicking range, comfortable though basic in punching range, and completely at a loss in grappling range. A fifth Dan Karataka is a white belt grappler. Many of the basic blocks and stances are good for building a strong body and spirit, but are of little direct use in real combat. Much of the training, depending of course on the instructor, is unrealistic and largely inapplicable. The biggest fault with traditional training, certainly in this decade, and this applies to most other martial arts, is the lack of communication and honesty between instructor and student. The student needs to be told exactly how it is, how and why a *live* situation is going to make them feel scared shitless, that some of the big, slow movements that they practice are not recommended for the real deal. Most instructors will not or cannot pass on the kind of enlightenment a student needs if he's going to survive in such a savage arena. Some of the top martial arts instructors in the world have little or no real fighting experience, so they are not in a good position to teach what they (do not) know to others. All they can teach is how they think it might be. I'm not saying that it makes them bad instructors of their art, on the contrary, they may be great instructors, but you can't teach what you don't know.

Due to the fact that grappling is not allowed during sparring, sloppy technique is inadvertently encouraged: slowly retracted kicks, over-committed kicks, unrealistically high and flash kicks, pivoting on one leg after retraction of the kick, leg fencing (both fighters standing on one leg and fencing with their feet), deep stances that impede fast movement, low or no guard that leaves the major target (the head) completely unprotected, only using straight punches and constantly pulling those punches on impact with the target, not practising any grappling and lastly being frightened of admitting that Karate does have weaknesses for fear of offending their art, instructors, masters or even themselves and getting deeply offended by anyone else that has the insight to point out the weaknesses to them.

Gung fu

This is very similar to Karate in that it teaches more kicking than punching, with the exception of Wing chun and one or two other systems which do teach close range techniques, but again no, or very little, grappling. They are often guilty of believing that they have an art that does not need to practice ground fighting and theirs is the ultimate art. There is no such thing and such thoughts are, at best naive. Similarly little pressure testing is done to really test and perfect technique. Those that normally manage to make these arts complete are the instructors who have a wealth of experience behind them in other systems such as wrestling and judo, or boxing.

Animal Day

Judo and Wrestling
Both are now predominantly sports, and out of all the systems that I have practiced these were definitely the most demanding. They pressure test severely but again only within the periphery of their own rules. Whilst in grappling range these exponents are definitely potentate, whilst out of range, they are like ducks out of water, though it has to be said that in match fighting, which is very different from street fighting, they definitely rule.

Aikido
In general this is a very restrictive to the average player because it is almost (if not totally) defensive. The top men in this art may make it work in a live situation, but I don't see it being effective for the average player. The best means of defence, without a shadow of a doubt, is attack. Anything long winded and over technical is of little use as street fights are over in anything from one to five seconds. Its practice in the majority of dojos is totally unrealistic, the attacks that are thrown to practice defence are benign and completely out of context with the real world of violence. As an art I find Aikido beautiful, as a self-defence I find it sadly misdirected. Some of the basic locks are nice as a part of the support system, but that is about all I can find, as far as self-defence is concerned, of any worth.

Thai Boxing
What a ferocious art. Thai is one of the few systems that nearly has it all and no one can doubt the power of the techniques. The punching in Thai is not so good as in Western boxing, but it is a lot better than any of the other systems. Its only real flaw is vertical and especially horizontal grappling.

In vertical grappling Thai is good though slightly unrealistic, not in its power or technique but more in the fact that, because it does not allow ground fighting, the exponents are too vertical and so easy to take to the floor by a system that does allow ground fighting. The atemi in vertical fighting is very strong and very effective, in reality it would be very difficult to apply the same techniques to someone who is not fighting to Thai rules. Vertical grappling, in a real situation is usually only there for a fleeting moment before it goes to ground. Against someone with knowledge a Thai boxer, the same as other trained or untrained fighters, would be taken quickly to ground.

Ju-Jitsu

As yet I have not seen any Ju-jitsu that has really impressed me, except for one or two people like Dave Turton and Trev Roberts who are exceptional, and of course who can dispute the indomitable Gracie family in America. More generally, though, Ju-jitsu tends again to be too defensive, *when the opponent attacks we defend with…etc.* Defence has to be addressed because it is not always possible to read a situation and be *first,* but when 99% of what you teach relies on having to wait for the attacker to attack, something seems acutely amiss, and when it comes to fighting numbers this strategy is absolute suicide and will not work. Also, with few exceptions, all the techniques are practised against designated attacks and with compliancy, pressure from training is sadly missing. Many Ju-jitsu practitioners tend also to lean heavily to grappling, this is fine in the one on one fight but problematic in numbers fighting where it is difficult to grapple more than one attacker at the same time, several of my friends have been stabbed by the friends or girlfriends of the person that they are tied up with, also grappling range is unique in that once sought it can seldom be changed for another more suitable, you are held there by the grip on your adversity. I also find that a lot of the Ju-Jitsu systems no longer include randori (free fighting), this is what takes the teeth out of it really, if they re-introduce this I think there would be a marked difference.

The concept of throwing an assailant cleanly and then moving on to a second attacker is also rarely viable because most attackers pull the thrower to the floor when they are thrown. Consider this fact: 9 out of 10 fights start at punching range. How much time do you in your system designate to the practice of accurate and powerful close range punching? If you can't get impact on a bag or pads in the controlled environment it is hugely unlikely that you will suddenly miraculously develop those attributes when a situation becomes *live*. I'm amazed by the amount of people, many of a very high grade, that can't generate impact or power when it comes to hitting a training implement.

Most of my training revolves around punching because I know from experience that that is where it is going to happen. So if your system doesn't involve a lot of punching, think again.

Western Boxing
Western boxing is definitely the best whilst in punching range and every session is a severe pressure test, again within its own rules, but in kicking and grappling range it comes a very sorry second place. However, these boxers are so deft with their hands that it rarely ever gets to the other ranges.

A boxer with knowledge of other fighting systems is a very dangerous person. Real fights mostly start at punching range and, if the puncher is a good one, end there also. For this reason, if I had the choice of only one art for the physical aspect of self-defence it would be boxing, if I had the choice of two arts it would be boxing and wrestling/Judo. If I had the choice of three it would be boxing, wrestling and Thai.

The street fighter
What helps the street fighter swim clear of the maelstrom of trained fighters is that they lack very little. Every technique they use has been tried and tested in live situations. They can kick, punch and grapple like they were born to do it. Most trained fighters are still embryos in the womb of combat whilst the street fighter is fully matured. They control the *duck syndrome* with consummate ease and put most opponents out of the fight before they even know they are in it. They are fighting chameleons, adapting themselves to any given situation and changing their fight plan to better any fighter. If they are facing a fighter that is or appears to be a bit *handy* they may act weak or scared so as to mentally disarm them, then strike out fiercely when least expected to. If the opponent looks as though he may have a chink in his mental armour, the fighter may act over confident or strong to psyche him out and back him down, thus winning with out the use of violence, or, if and when necessary, a combination of them both.

When fighting has commenced the street fighter will, if he has not already finished the fight, assess the opponent's artillery automatically and fight them at their weakest range, forcing a kicker to punch or a puncher to kick or a puncher and kicker to grapple etc.

More than anything the street fighter will use guile as opposed to force, his main artillery will be dialogue, this is used to prime, disarm and psyche out the opponent. His power base will be deception and innate cunning. He may go through and win several hundred encounters with only one or two techniques, beating the man with hundreds of techniques up his sleeve whilst he is in mental log jam trying to figure out which of the hundreds he should apply. He will also use everything in his environment as an incidental weapon.

His weakness lies in the fact that he is usually a five second fighter, every second beyond that and the fight goes more and more against him. The one or two techniques that he so favours at each range will be quickly exhausted and the stamina that he has not got will disappear at a rate of knots. Because he is so unused to anyone going the distances and the fact that he is feeling the excruciating pain of oxygen debt (this comes when the stamina goes) he will often panic at this stage and his bottle may start to go. It may take a minute to get him in this state, though, and that minute may be the longest that you ever experience.

So try to be honest when evaluating yourself and your system. If you can't do that you will not even be able to get on the first rung of the ladder.

Chapter Four

An Introduction to the Inner Opponent

We have already spoken about the inner opponent. You will all have had to come to terms with him at some stage of your training. In this short chapter I would just like to introduce him in case anyone out there thinks that he does not exist, or perhaps can not quite comprehend what I mean by inner opponent. I will list a few exercises that I would like you to do, the reasons for this are twofold, one is to allow you to hear the voice of negativity and the other is to allow you to see how much control you have over him at this present time.

If you find yourself giving in very early and unable to control the inner opponent then it is fair to say that you are not in control of the inner opponent. Obviously that will revert the more you confront and overcome him.

I shall try to list several different exercises in the hope that I will find one that you do not like or are not comfortable with, don't choose the easy ones that would be defeating the object. You must look at the list and choose the hardest exercise, for you. If they are all too easy then choose one of your own that is hard. I would also like you to do the exercise for the next three days, this will allow the inner opponent to try and weaken you in anticipation. Whichever exercise you do try, do it to failure - that is until you can no longer physically do one more repetition. This doesn't mean when the inner opponent tells you to stop, it means when you cannot physically manage one more second or repetition.

Animal Day

When the inner opponent does click in, this may happen before you even start the exercise, especially on the second and third day. Try to override him and continue for as long as you can.

These are the stages where he will click in, depending upon your fitness and control; The way to control the inner opponent is detailed in chapter two, **Understanding Yourself**, and in greater detail in *Fear - the friend of exceptional people*.

Anticipation

When there is anticipation of adversity, boredom, pain etc the inner opponent will click in and try to get you to abort, 'Why are you doing this to yourself?' he will ask, 'you don't need this, you've got nothing to prove.' This is especially so when there is a time lapse between anticipation and confrontation. This is when he can be at his most destructive because he has time to wear you down and talk you out of the confrontation. Your most vulnerable time will be when your mind is not occupied.

Pre-confrontation

Many people get right to the door of confrontation and then fail to open it, the inner opponent taking one final deceptive swipe to force abortion.

In-confrontation

You have actually faced confrontation and are within it when the inner opponent strikes again, first at:

Boredom

'Oh this is getting boring, I've had enough, I'm calling it a day.'

Second at:

Pain
'Crikey, this is hurting, can't be good for me, I'm going to stop. I think I've done enough'.

Thirdly:

Exhaustion
'Give in . . . give in . . . give in.'

Fourthly:

Nausea
'I can't bear to go on. I feel like I'm dying. What am I doing here? I don't need this.'

And lastly:

Afterwards
'O.K. you've proved that you can do it, that's enough now, you don't need to do any more.'

As we said earlier, look out for the inner opponent, the excuses and the cop-outs, they will materialise and must be overcome. Here are the exercises, chose the hardest one for you and try to go to failure, obviously I don't want anyone to physically injure themselves so just do as much as you can without making yourself ill.

Animal Day

1) Roman chair

Sit, as per illustration, with your back against the wall in a seated position with your knees bent at a 90 degree angle (parallel to the floor), let your arms lay limply by your side and be sure not to put your hands on your legs for support, also make sure that you have the correct angle, don't cheat yourself, if your knees are bent to much or not enough the pressure is taken away from the thighs and the exercise is wasted.

2) Step ups

Stand in front of a chair or bench, as per illustration, at about your own knee height, place your hands on your head (or by your side) and step up and down for as many repetitions as you can. Keep your hands on your head at all times.

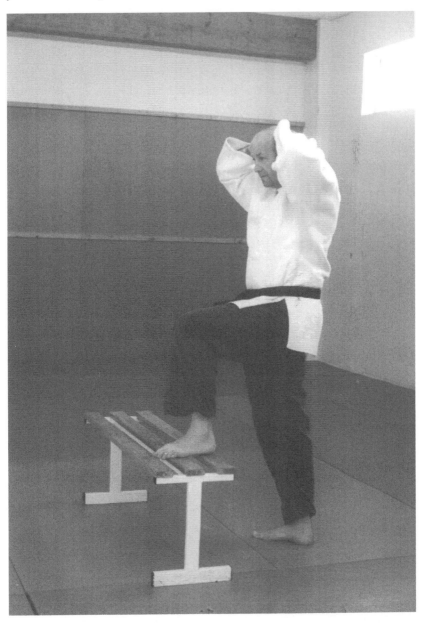

Animal Day

3) Wind sprints

Stand at one end of a room about 50 feet long and sprint to one end and then back. Go back and forth for thirty seconds, you must sprint as fast as you can. At the end of the thirty seconds rest for 15 seconds before repeating the same exercise for 25 seconds, 15 seconds rest, sprint for twenty seconds, 15 seconds rest, then sprint for 20 seconds and 15 seconds rest then finally sprint for 10 seconds.

If you feel like slowing down towards the end of the sprint, or for that matter at any time during the sprint make sure that you do not.

4) Running

If you are already a good runner this exercise will not be a good one for you, chose one that you are not good at or at least unaccustomed to.

Go out for a run and go as far as you can, see which goes first, your stamina or your will.

5) Fart-legging

The same as with running only with fart-legging you should run 100 yds and then sprint 100 yds with no rest in between.

6) Staggered press-ups

Make a press-up position, as per illustration, make sure that your back is straight. Lower your body down until your chest is just touching, but not resting on the floor. Hold for the count of five seconds and then push back up to the start position. Repeat the process for as many reps as you can before your arms give way.

7) Star jump-burpees

From a standing position, jump high in the air and spread your arms and legs like a star, as you land go into a crouch position and shoot your legs out backwards so that you are in a press up position then shoot them back to the crouch position and stand back up, as per illustration. With out pause or rest repeat the exercise from star jump to burpee. Do as many as you can.

Animal Day

8) Pull ups

Hanging from a bar or doorframe with your palms facing forward pull yourself up until the back of your neck touches the bar/frame, then lower back to the start position, make sure that you do not rest your feet on the floor. Repeat as many as you can. When you've done as many as you can, have a ten second break and do as many as you can again, then a ten second break and as many as you can for a third and final time.

If there is nothing here that you find demanding enough use some thing of your own invention, as long as it incites the inner opponent into action. What these exercises will do is allow you to see the inner opponent on a more tangible level. This allows you then to recognise him when you come to confront Animal Day itself, and also when he pops up in other aspects of your life. By stepping into adversity and summoning up the inner opponent we allow ourselves practice in fighting him. So next time you want a sparring session, don't ring up a mate, summon up the inner opponent. If you can control him you can achieve anything.

As they say (whoever they are), real power is not getting others to do as you want, it is getting ourselves to do what we want.

Chapter Five

The Progressive Pyramid

If you have read any of my previous books (if you haven't, why haven't you?) you will know that I like pyramids because they allow a steady build up to a desired goal. So rather than just jump in the deep end and have Animal Day you can build up to it in pyramidic stages, the same as you would when attempting to lift heavyweights in the gym. You wouldn't try to lift three hundred pounds on the first lift, you would pyramid your weight, gradually increasing the poundage so that your body and mind can get used to handling progressively more weight until you reach the desired three hundred pounds. We shall do this by practising restricted sparring, restricted in content and restricted in control, progressing eventually to no restrictions and no-control, this being Animal Day itself. Bear in mind though that Animal Day is anything that places you under pressure, if the thought of putting on the gloves and doing three rounds with a boxer scares the pants off you then that's Animal Day.

I would like to break this down into categories that will work for you irrespective of what style you practice, some of the exercises will favour your particular system and others will not, it is important that you do all the prescribed exercises and not miss the ones that you don't like. If you do that you will have wasted your time. The whole premise is based on being uncomfortable, that's where the growth is, if you are comfortable you are already stagnant.

The first thing will be totally to isolate the different distances and practice them within slight restrictions, then later to intermingle them with less and less restriction until you reach the stage where anything goes. Here are the stages:

• Chapter six: *grappling*.
This involving vertical and horizontal grappling, atemi, biting etc.

• Chapter seven: *punching*.
This involving long range, mid range and close range boxing and eventually elbows.

• Chapter eight: *kicking*.
This involving long and short range kicking, stomping and independent sweeping.

• Chapter nine: *weapons fighting*.
Sparring with a variety of weapons with unrehearsed attacks using either marker pens as knifes or other pretend weapons.

• Chapter ten: *combining distances*.
Restricted sparring combining all ranges.

• Chapter eleven: *Animal Day*.

With weapons and without. For obvious reasons the weapons cannot be real all though the empty hand techniques will be full contact. With my own people we wear gloves for the standing work so that you can hit as hard as you like, similar to boxing or Thai, if the fight hits the floor we strip the gloves off the fighters so that they can use the grips necessary for grappling. Because of the inherent dangers of bare knuckle fighting we restrict the floor blows to slaps. This is necessary; if you don't have some restrictions the injuries will be catastrophic.

Whatever your art it should fall into one of these categories, the weapons chapter is really for the Aikido people and those that think their art is competent in weapons defence. No matter what your art you should go through all of the chapters and try to make what you know work for you and if it doesn't work find some thing that does.

Chapter Six

Grappling

Grappling, to the majority that does not practice the art, will be the most demanding of all the endeavours next to Animal Day itself and should be practised with great caution using a matted area and acquiring a good knowledge of how to break fall. The tap system should be observed at all times. If an opponent taps himself, the floor or his opponent this will signify submission and the opponent should release the hold immediately. For added safety always practice in no less than threes so that a third party will be able to observe in case one of the fighters gets into trouble and for whatever reason is unable to tap submission.

Biting

Animal Day

Are you shocked by the fact that I have included biting in this text? If you are then you are unprepared for a real encounter. Many fighters – like it or not – initiate their attack with a bite, some use it instinctively to finish an opponent. If you are not at the very least apt in defending against the bite then the chances are you will be beaten by the first person that uses this technique. The only way to learn bite-defense is to include biting in your sparring. Many of the techniques that you now practice will have to change when the bite is included, anything that is left anywhere near the teeth of a determined attacker will be bitten to the bone, even severed, I know of many fighters who have had noses and ears bitten clean off. Some of the more callous fighters out there will also either swallow the ear/nose after biting it off or stamp on the severed article after spitting it out so that a surgeon is unable to stitch it back on again. There will also be occasions- it has happened to me – where your only way of surviving a situation is to attack your aggressor with a bite. You may choose not to, for what ever reason, and that is your prerogative, but if you do you will lose and maybe even die. If you find the thought of biting some one repugnant and feel you will never be able to do it, include the biting into your curriculum anyway, just so that you can learn to defend against it.

When biting an opponent in gym fighting one should bite and release, only applying enough force to let the opponent know that he has been bitten. Don't try to get a submission with a bite, it is enough to know that in a real situation the bite would probably have secured you the victory.

Butting

It is an important part of your curriculum that you learn to butt, when the distance is right, as an instinct.

Again, in the real world a good butt can finish a fight, if you receive the butt it may finish you so it is good, in training, not only to practice attacking with a butt, but also defending against the same. It is not always necessary to use full contact with the head, it can be a little too devastating in the controlled environment, unless your opponent is wearing protective head gear. Personally I use just enough force to let my opponent know that he has been caught so that he'll know better the next time.

Gouging

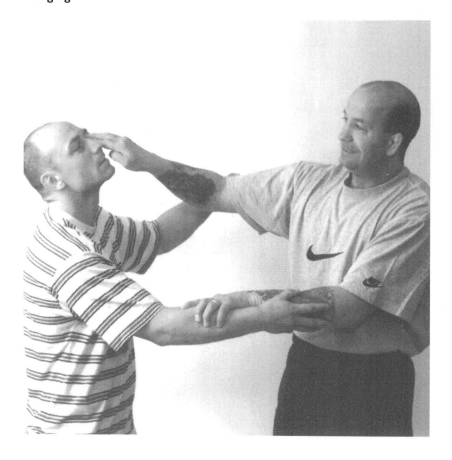

I do put pressure on the eyes when sparring but I never inflict damage by scraping and gauging, this could easily blind your opponent. It is imperative though that you learn to defend against eye attacks in grappling so they must be included, again with control.

Grappling again will be split into stages. Try to become familiar with all the different aspects before you join them together; they are as follows.

Vertical grappling
This will be split into bulling, just atemi, clean throwing without atemi, defending, attacking, all out vertical grappling.

Ground work
This will be split into pins and hold-downs with and without atemi, escapes with and without atemi and all out ground fighting.

All-out grappling
Combining vertical and horizontal grappling.

I will take vertical grappling first. Because this is not a book about technique please refer to my other books, if you have no prior knowledge, for relevant techniques to employ in all the different sections. For the time that you go all out I recommend that you use some sort of protective gear.

Vertical grappling

Bulling
Hold your opponent in any grip you wish and pull each other around with force, not trying to throw or strike, just control the grip, the person who controls the grip is usually the person who controls the fight. A good hold for bulling is the wrestlers hold of neck and arm (as illus). This exercise will help you to become familiar with a grappling embrace and help develop a good steady stance. It also helps the practitioners get used to being touched or mauled, many people feel very restricted, threatened and even claustrophobic when being grabbed. Get familiar with this before moving on to the next step.

Animal Day

Bulling

Just atemi

From any grip you can get on your opponent, look for possible strikes with the head, knees, feet, hands etc. Still not looking to throw the opponent and using good control with the strikes. This will allow you to see how difficult it is to strike once in vertical grappling. If you think that you may be able to use trapping, try it here. Slowly build up the speed and lessen the control until you are going all out. Once you are going all out don't let the opponent do anything that you don't want him to do. In all-out there is no compliancy, if a technique or concept is good it will work on its own merits.

Practice throwing techniques with a partner, under compliant conditions and without atemi. Building up to throwing without compliancy. Once you feel comfortable with this concept add semi-controlled atemi.

Defence/attack practice

One side practices defence whilst the other side practices attack, starting off with a little partner resistance and building up to full partner resistance.

All out vertical grappling

Vertical grappling with no partner compliancy, anything vertical goes right through to throwing to the ground position. When the fight hits the floor stop and start again. Do not, at this stage fight on the floor.

Animal Day

Ground Work

Light free fighting
Starting from a kneeling position fight off, very lightly, and have a good feel of ground fighting. No pressure is intended here so enjoy it, don't let it progress to anything heavy. In light free fighting you and your partner should both be looking for an opening for pins, hold downs, escapes etc. No atemi at this stage. This exercise is purely for feeling and getting sensitised with the distance.

Pins and hold downs

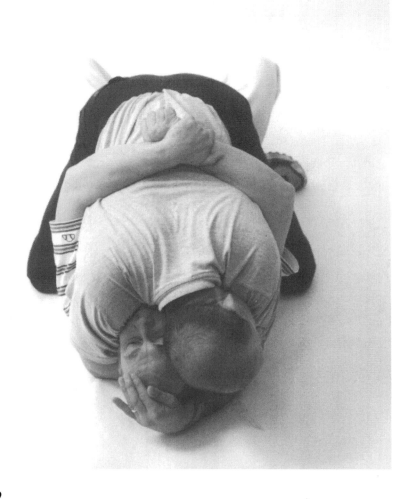

Practice pinning or holding down your opponent, initially with a little partner resistance and progressing to full partner resistance. Start by choosing a specific technique, hold your partner down with it and then let him try and break the hold with you trying to keep him pinned. At the beginning stage do not use any atemi but gradually build up to its inclusion.

Escapes

Practice escape techniques from a pinned position. Start with a little partner resistance and no atemi building up to full partner resistance and include atemi.

All-out ground fighting

Anything goes, on the ground. Fighting with full partner resistance until submission. The only restriction that the fight stays on the floor, no standing at this stage..

All-out light grappling

Anything goes from vertical to ground fighting with the restriction of control. To start and build familiarity, go light.

All-out heavy grappling

All-out, anything goes with the range of grappling. No atemi should be used outside of grappling range, restrict yourself to working only within the pin-submission rules.

Whilst the former (and the forthcoming) will help you build up to Animal Day it is also an excellent method of dissecting and practising the separate aspects of each distance, it is the way I still practice now, in between Animal Days. It will develop a comprehensive appreciation of every distance and also allow you to perfect and develop new techniques. The best way to learn a distance correctly is to isolate it from the other distances and practice every aspect, then bring it back into the full curriculum.

Chapter Seven

Punching

Punching is the main artillery range so I spend more time on the punching arts than I do any other distance, it is certainly the most important range when it comes to a real fight.

Again we will isolate the different aspects of punching so as to perfect each and also to pyramid the intensity up to full contact boxing.

Note:

If the puncher gets close enough it would be a natural extension to use the elbows as opposed to the fists. Certainly in the unrestricted sections it is viable to try and employ the elbows in with the hands if and when possible.

Punch isolation (on the bag)

Each punch should be isolated and practised on its own, this can be worked in sparring or on the bag/pads etc. To start with, use a training implement like the bag or pads and work three 2 minute rounds just on that one punch. Starting with the jab, then the cross (right or left depending upon your stance) left hook, right hook, left uppercut, right uppercut. It is important here that you do restrict your practice to one punch, don't be tempted to throw a cross if you are practising a jab etc.

Punch isolation (in light-heavy sparring)

Exactly the same as above but with a partner. This is called restricted sparring (use boxing gloves), restricted to only one punch, i.e. jab or cross etc. You may use either side to defend. Keep it light and enjoy it, at this level you should be learning to use the different punches against a partner who is doing the same. Because you are both going light and there is no danger of being hurt you will feel more comfortable trying out new moves, if you spar too heavy too soon the learning process will be greatly impeded, you will be very unlikely to try out anything new if you know that you will get hurt should it fail.

Progress to heavy restricted sparring.

One side restricted sparring

Right cross against opponent

Animal Day

This time you are restricted to attacking with only one side of the body, though you may defend with both sides. The restriction may be left hand attacks only or right hand attacks only, you can also have one side attacking only left side whilst the other attacks only right, or vice-versa, or both sides using only right side or both partners using only left side. Be sure to agree on the restriction before commencing the fight to avoid confusion.

Defence/attack only

One side defending whilst the other side attacks, starting light with no restrictions on what technique you use (as long as it is a punching technique), then swap around so that the attacker defends and the defender attacks. Build up, very gradually until the attacks are full contact. Again, it is important not to break your restriction, if you are defending make sure that you do not counter attack. Restrict yourself purely to blocking or evasion.

Light hand sparring

Sparring with no technique restriction but with a strict restriction on control, start of very lightly.

All-out hand sparring

Anything goes hand sparring with no restriction on technique or control. Do not let it progress into kicking or grappling. Hands only. You can use any technique, it is not restricted to boxing punches, if you want to attempt say a spinning back-fist etc. feel free.

As with the grappling the former exercises are a good way of training for excellence in hands, isolate each aspect and polish it before replacing it into the curriculum.

Chapter Eight

Kicking

Although kicking is the weakest of the main artillery ranges it is still important, it cannot be slighted. It is especially effective when attacking/finishing a felled opponent or kicking a second/third opponent when/if your hands are tied up in grappling the first opponent. If kicks are to be employed they should be ferocious, accurate and powerful, there is no sense in throwing a kick, or any technique for that matter, that does not damage the adversary. Again this means training for contact and not for points. If the foot is taken off the floor and employed as an attack it should do the damage and then be replaced to the floor again as quickly as possible. The most vulnerable targets, attacking a vertical opponent, are the lower abdomen, pubic bone, genitals, thighs, knees and shins (ankles and feet if using stamping kicks). Anything above the waist is less vulnerable and dangerous to the kicker.

I will break the kicking down it to separate fragments.

Isolated kicking on the bag/pads

Animal Day

As with the punching it is necessary to isolate the kicking technique in order to perfect it. Front kick, side kick, round house, back kick etc. should be practised on the bags/pads/strike shield individually for three two minute rounds aiming for power, speed and accuracy. Make sure that you don't get into the habit of leaving the kicking leg out to long or pivoting on the support leg after connection with the target. Power and speed will not just come on its own, if you want to kick faster or harder you must try to kick faster and harder. Practice the kicks at different ranges.

All-out kicking (on the bag/pads)
Any kick on the bag/pads/kick shield etc. Go for power and fast retraction, vary the distance.

Isolated kicking: with a partner

The same as above, only now sparring with a partner. Which ever kick you choose be it front kick or round house etc, use both legs and spar with your partner who is doing the same. Start off light and build up until you are using full contact kicks. You may also mix and match the techniques, for instance you attack only front kick and you partner only side kick, or you attack round house whilst your partner attacks front kick etc.

All-out kicking (with a partner)

Kick sparring with no restrictions on technique or power. Start off light and gently build up to full contact.

If you want to develop excellent kicking technique isolate each kick and work it to distraction, then join it back in with the other techniques.

Chapter Nine

Weapons Fighting

Weapons fighting is a very specialised area, I have been faced with weapons on the pavement on a few occasions, I have been glassed three times, attacked with bottles, threatened with guns etc (and that's just by my ex-wife). Being faced by a weapon in the controlled arena is worlds apart from facing a thug with a knife in the REAL arena. Most of the knife defence systems that I have witnessed simply wouldn't work in the real world.

From my experience with knives a stabber never shows and a shower never stabs. If someone really wants to stab you he will not show the blade and if he only wants to scare you he will show the blade. Knife attacks are usually ferocious, frenzied and fired under the veil of mass deception. In this chapter all I want to highlight is the reality of knife attack by weapon-sparring with absolutely no partner compliancy. Use old clothes and a marker pen (if you are caught the pen will mark your clothes and show you where you have been hit). With the edged blade being the most dangerous of the weapons (probably even more so than the gun) we will restrict this chapter to use of the blade, I would, however, recommend that you spar with other simulated weapons to gain familiarity and gain a little realism.

Note:
Be sure not to fall into compliancy here, it will be easy to allow your partner to use techniques from your (or his) own system out of habit, or because you don't want to offend him by highlighting

the weaknesses in his system or technique. There will be no room for that here.

Weapon attack sparring

One opponent defending, the other attacking with a marker pen. The attacker should try to catch the opponent as many times as he can within three minutes, using any technique and with no restriction on control. At the end of the three minutes change around so that the defender attacks and the attacker defends. At the end of the three minutes count the marks on eachother's clothes and body to see who was the most successful in defence and attack.

Don't cheat yourself or your partner by throwing halfhearted attacks or by being a compliant opponent, in defence or attack. Mark your partner as many times during the three minutes as you can.

Weapons contest sparring

Face your partner with your marker pens at the ready and fight with no restrictions on technique or control. Fight three three-minute rounds with 30 seconds rest in between. At the end of the three rounds count the amount of pen marks on eachother's body and clothes, the one carrying the most marks is the loser.

None of this is worth practising unless there is intent in the attacker, make your attacks committed and ferocious, even frenzied. Compliancy will not highlight weakness so do not be compliant.

This practice is an excellent acid test of whether your knife/weapons defence is or is not sound. If it is an effective system it will work here, if it is not, it will not. A system that only works under certain conditions or certain rules will crumble badly under the pressure of the real deal. So if it does not work here, under manufactured pressure, don't kid yourself that it will work outside. Re-evaluate the system that you are learning and make any changes that need making.

Chapter Ten

Combining Distances

In this chapter, the penultimate before Animal Day, we will combine distances. This is the last preparatory step before going all-out, it is also an excellent way of forcing practitioners to fight at a distance they do not like or understand. This is often necessary when dealing with people who avoid certain distances.

Many practitioners of a given distance lose against other fighters of different distances simply because they are ignorant to that distance. This chapter will force everyone at any distance to learn defence and attack against others at a foreign range. For instance, I would class punching distance as a more dangerous range than kicking, yet I have beaten many good boxers in the street with a kicking technique because they did not know how to defend against my kicks. Many grapplers are badly hurt as they close the gap with punchers because they have no defence in their system against a puncher.

The combinations here are endless and you can mix or match as you please. I shall list here a few that are practised at my own club.

Note:
All should be practiced lightly to start and then built up to full contact. When contact is unrestricted elbow attacks would be allowed.

Boxer

1) Boxer against a kicker

One person is restricted to the use of hand techniques whilst the other is restricted to the use of kicking techniques though both may defend without restriction. This will allow/force a weak puncher/kicker to punch or kick, it will also allow/force a strong kicker/puncher to test is skills against a kicker/puncher.

2) Boxer against a grappler

One person is restricted to the use of hand techniques, the other restricted to the use of grappling techniques allowing or forcing both to fight against an opponent of a different range.

3) Boxer against all-out

One person is restricted to hand techniques only whilst the other is completely unrestricted, allowing the boxer to test against all-out and the *all-out* to test against a boxer.

Kicker

1) Kicker against a boxer

Trying at all times to keep himself in kicking range and the boxer out of punching range.

2) Kicker against a grappler

Trying to keep the grappler at bay and not allowing him to get close enough to grab (a hard task).

3) Kicker against all-out
Trying to maintain kicking range and stop the all-out opponent at the same range.

Grappler

1) Grappler against boxer
The grappler has to get inside punching range and take the puncher to the floor.

2) Grappler against kicker
The grappler has to get inside kicking and punching range and take the kicker to the floor.

3) Grappler against all-out
The grappler has to get inside punching and kicking range and take the opponent to the floor.

This is the last step, now you should be ready to fight all-out against all-out, this being Animal Day.

Even when you get used to Animal Day you should still practice all the isolation and restriction exercises to perfect each element of each distance. Animal Day is not something that you need to do every session, perhaps once every two weeks or once every month.

All the exercises in the forgoing chapters can be spread over as long a period as you wish and certainly used as a regular training method. It involves contact at every level, initially the contact will probably be unnerving but in the long term you will get used to it and it will seem very ordinary. You can get used to anything if you do it often enough.

Chapter Eleven

Animal Day

Many people I speak to think that Animal Day is an extreme, I think it is just ordinary, but that's because I have been doing it for so long now, once you are used to it you will feel this way too. As well as perfecting technique and testing concepts Animal Day is a great mind builder: coping with mental adversity builds the mind like bar bell curls build the biceps. If you can do it and continue to do it you will become a very strong individual, this strength will overflow into your every day life and make you someone to be reckoned with (if you are not already). Eventually it will give you the confidence to transcend the physical and - as I said earlier – let people off. Ultimately you should be so good, so confident that you give the physical stuff the big heave-ho, you sack it and start looking for higher echelon ways to solve your problems. You also start looking for less transient means of building yourself up. Any physical ability is, at best, just a way to get you into cerebral arena, at worst it will enable you to protect you body until that time arrives. If you are still at the stage where you secretly long for an attack just so that you can prove your ability, then you have no ability at all; when you are scared to use your skills because they are so potent, then you are getting there. But that is a different book entirely.

The confidence gained from testing your physical/psychological wares is mostly due to your internal battles with the inner opponent. If you can control him in combat then you can certainly control him in your every day life where he wants to, and usually does, rule supreme. The adversity of standing up to yourself will give you a greater appreciation of the finer things in life. People like Gandhi developed supreme internal power by fighting the inner opponent, and he never picked up a weight, never got on the mat, never punched the bag, he developed an indemonstrable spirit with the practice of abstainism; abstaining from certain food groups, fasting, abstaining from negative thought etc. He completely by-passed fighting (in fact he was a pacifist) and developed an iron will by fighting himself (or certainly by fighting his own addictions) on a daily basis. In the end he even gave up sex in his bid for better-dom (a bloke can go too far I think). But, again, that is another book too.

When I've run five miles and done 20-40 rounds on the bag believe me when I tell you that a cup of tea is a cup of tea, it tastes like nectar, your food tastes nicer, your wife sweeter your children more fun and life seems bliss. After adversity, Animal Day or a good training session, you feel as though you have earned every thing that you get, the strength of mind gained also helps you to cope a lot better with the stresses of life.

People think nothing of going to the toilet every day and getting rid of the physical waste of the day, but what about the mental waste that lies fermenting in our bodies and minds? The guy that cut you up in the car this morning, the boss at work that doesn't appreciate you, in fact he treats you like shit, your ex-wife/husband who still tries to dominate your life, all of the things in society that add to the psychological waste that we carry around and do not de-sludge. Training, Animal Day etc can be a mental de-sludge, a way to excrete all of the stresses of the day so that we do not come home from another bad day at work and take it out on our spouse or our children, the people close to us. So as well as all of the formerly

Animal Day

mentioned benefits of a solid training routine we also get rid of unwanted psychological waste.

Animal Day should not be taken too lightly, it can be dangerous and I highly recommend that you use protective equipment, as I have said though in my other books (you should read them you know) if there was no risk there would be no point, you would only be getting some thing that everyone else can get, it needs to be hard so that only the elite few who are prepared to sacrifice, will achieve. Between those that dream and those that do is a cavernous hole called risk, only those that dare to step across that gap will achieve and those that do not will remain forever dreamers. Pain/fear is what keeps people ordinary, and there is nothing wrong with ordinary if that is what you want from life, if you want to be somebody then you have to take pain on board and learn to handle it.

I digress, Animal Day can be broken down into two parts: Timed and limitless.

Timed Animal Day

Time your rounds, this will give you a light at the end of the tunnel if things are feeling or getting a little ugly. Start with three 1 minute rounds and then build up to two minute rounds and then three minute rounds. Depending upon your fitness build up the number of rounds that you do, try to get up to 8-10 rounds, if you can't cope with that many stick at 3-5 rounds.

Limitless

In limitless Animal Day you fight until knock-out or submission, that's how it would be in a real fight (or certainly until there is a winner and a loser).

Even though you have now gone through all of the different ranges you will still have a favourite distance, everyone does, so when you fight off it is your prerogative to stick at that range if you so desire (if you can).

Ultimately your goal should be to become competent/good/ excellent at all ranges, this will allow you to take others that are not competent at each range to their weakest range. So in theory every fight that you have in the gym/dojo will be different, if your partner is a better grappler than you, you should try to avoid grappling and fight him at kicking and punching range, if he is a better puncher than you, you should be avoiding punching range and fighting him at kicking or grappling range, if he is a better kicker than you then avoid kicking range and fight him at punching or grappling range.

Similarly if he is better at two ranges than you, kicking and punching for instance, then you would be looking to fight him at, his weakest range, grappling etc.

If you face an opponent who is better than you at all three ranges then you should try to take him to the weakest part of any given range, for instance in boxing range you have good attacking fighters who are not very good defensively, so you would take the fight to him where he is weakest, in defence, or he might be a good close range puncher but a poor long range puncher, so fight him at long range.

Even on a psychological level you may take a fighter to a weak point, even if they best you at all physical ranges. For instance, I watched a British heavyweight kick-boxing champion sparring with a guy that was out punching and out kicking him (there was no grappling allowed due to full contact rulings) so the heavyweight champion added a little mental pressure by allowing a bit of anger to show and by constantly moving into his opponents techniques as though they were not hurting him (even though they were). Within a about a minute and a half the British champion was all over his sparring partner because he was starting to bottle out. A combination of displayed anger, made the opponent believe that the fight was going to become real, and no show of pain or emotion, made the opponent believe that the attacker was either impervious to feeling or that his own techniques were not having any effect. So a better fighter was beaten on a mental level.

This of course happens all of the time in real situations on a street level, good fighters lose against bad fighters because their weakest link is mental as opposed to physical. I have used this psyching out process, in and out of the dojo, on many occasions, in fact I'd go as far as to say that I have won more fights with the use of psyche than I have with the use of force. If you look at the world of professional boxing you will see mass evidence of this. Pre-fight, in-fight and post-fight blurb. Intimidating the opponent at all levels and at all times before the fight, talking to him and beckoning him on during the fight (Ali was a master of in-fight blurb) and psyching the opponent out after the fight in preparation for a possible return fight (a classic of this is Nigel Benn and Chris Eubank). The pre-fight and post-fight also help to draw crowds to the fights. I will use Ali as a prime example, though the strategy can be worked on any level, in and out of combat, even sales men use the same kind of mind game to out gun possible rivals and even customers.

Pre-fight
Mohammed Ali was a master of intimidation before, during and after fights. As well as filling the stadium with fight fans and grossing

three or four times more money than any other heavyweight fighter of the time Ali's prime reason for using pre-fight blurb was to, 1) intimidate his opponent into thinking that he was unbeatable because of his blatant confidence, his words clicking off the opponents adrenalin and inner opponent, and thus using up valuable nervous energy. 2) Getting the opponent so angry that they use up masses of energy negatively before the fight so that when they reach the ring they have used up much of their fuel. 3) Getting the opponent so angry that he forgets his game plan because all he wants to do is teach this loud mouth a lesson that he won't forget.

In-fight

During the fight Ali would talk to his opponents and tell them what sissies they were and that their punches were weak and movement robotic and, 'hey, what the hell are you doing in the ring with a master like me? You're out of your league boy.' Again this would very often force anger, and thus wasted energy, in even the most experienced fighters, who would then abort their game plan to try and hurt Ali. A classic was the so-called *rope-a-dope* antics of the Ali/Foreman fight. Every round Ali would walk straight into the corner of the ring and lean his back on the ropes from where he would beckon Foreman on. For five rounds Foreman fell for the trap and tried with all his might to finish Ali. Ali took the best shots that Foreman could fire and then asked, whilst in the clinch, 'Is that the best you can do, you're a pussy, I thought you were supposed to be a hard hitter, my sister hits harder than that' etc.

Foreman forgot all of his well thought out game plans and went for the kill, after five rounds he was so mentally and physically exhausted that Ali knocked him out with what seemed like a glancing blow.

Animal Day

Post-fight

To rub salt into the wounds and enhance his unbeatable and fearless aura Ali would tell his opponents that next time it would be worse and that he'd rematch them *any time*. This would stick in the subconscious mind of the beaten opponent like a fish bone in the gullet.

Whenever I finished a *name* fighter I would always tell them, if they were conscious, (I'd tell their mates to tell them when they woke up if they were unconscious) that I would meet them for a return *any time, any place* and that next time I wouldn't take it so easy on them, after probably the beating of their lives that would leave them thinking, *he was taking it easy!*

When you are practising Animal Day don't worry if it gets scruffy, if you don't finish a fight in the street within the first couple of punches, scruffy is how it is going to get. As long as you are effective it does not matter how it looks, this is not a Kung-fu movie. Try and get a look at the fight scene at the end of the film *Lethal Weapon* where Mel Gibson fights the blond haired baddie (sorry I can't remember his name) that's how it gets when a fight has no restrictions. The ego takes a bit of a bashing when things stop looking aesthetic, but that is only because we have been conditioned by celluloid peer pressure to look clean and clinical against opponents that attack in order and fall theatrically to our counter-blows instead of hanging onto us like fighting parasites and *spoiling* our form (damn them). Real fighting, by nature is a scruffy affair, but once you understand and get a taste for it that scruffiness has an aesthetic look all of its own.

Don't give in: panic, pre-fight, in-fight and post-fight fear, exhaustion, nausea, pain and disorientation are all natural by-products of Animal

Day, do be unsettled by them, everyone, in varying degrees will feel them, what makes them more acceptable to the skeptical mind is the fact that they are all the same feelings that you will feel in a real confrontation and the only way you will ever get used to controlling them is by being exposed to them. Take heart, it does get better, the more you expose yourself to them the more desensitised you will get, so when the going gets tough, don't give in (or 'get going' as the song says).

It is usual at the start to want to give in very early on in the game, this again is usual so don't feel yourself a coward if you feel like, or even do, give in. The important thing is that each time you have an Animal Day you stretch that point more and more so that you learn to never give in.

Chokes, strangles and locks

Once these holds are firmly on there is little hope of escape, there is no point in letting your opponent take you to unconsciousness with a strangle rather than submit, neither is their a point in letting him break a limb because you are to stubborn to give in. If you can fight your way out of it, do so with as much vigour and cunning as possible and try to go as long as you can before *tapping out*, but if the hold is *on*, tap out and start again. If you are going to lose a fight the controlled environment is the place to do it, there should be no ego involved. There are certain elements that you will learn from losing that, unfortunately, can not be learned in any other way, so even losing holds its lessons and should be viewed under a positive light and not seen as the end of the world. If you are losing sleep because of one or two losses in the controlled arena then you have a problem with the ego, this has to be controlled or you will find the whole exercise becomes negative and learning will be slighted. When I first started boxing and wrestling I was losing a hell of a lot more than I was winning, I found it a very humbling experience, you should too.

Persevere

Initially, if you are not used to Animal Day, everything that you have learned before may seem or be out of sync. The distancing, timing, control, speed, power, attitude, intent will all be different. The suite of techniques you have sewn together over your years of training may not quite fit the frame of Animal Day (and therefore street scenario). Don't throw the suit away because it is not of immediate fit, tailor what you have to fit your new environment.

Many people say, after training with me, that they feel as though they have wasted their formative years in whatever system they have been studying, they haven't, far from it, everyone needs a base system to learn the fundamentals of kick, punch, block, footwork etc, and these element vary very little from style to style (contrary to what some may think). The problem with base builders is, that's all they do, build bases, rather they should set a good solid base and then build upon it. My base was Shotokan, on top of that base I built a solid construction of boxing, wrestling, Judo, Thai, gung-fu, weapons, ju-jitsu, weight training etc. What have you built upon your base, besides more and more bases? Your base system may be Thai or it may be Judo, or Gung-fu or whatever, it doesn't matter, you need a base and your upper elevations should compliment that base. If my base is Judo/wrestling then I would compliment that with boxing and/or Thai. If my base was Tae-kwodo I would compliment it with boxing and wrestling. Whatever my base is lacking or weak on I will add. Have a good look at what you've got and if it doesn't fit or change and/or add to it so that it does. Change is sense not sacrilege.

Epilogue

I class Animal Day as forge training, and as with any kind of forge training you don't have to do it for ever. I don't do Animal Day training (in a physical sense) any more. When you place a blade in the forge you only do it until the blade is tempered, then you take it out and for the rest of its life you keep the blade sharp, you don't place it back into the forge again. Once you have tempered your own blade (only you will know when this is) pull away from the forge and just keep the blade sharp. Animal Day is not forever; it is a stepping-stone to the higher echelons. It is my hope that once you have mastered Animal Day you will let go of this obsession (we all have) with being able to fight and move onto the finer things that life has to offer. My life is so exciting, there are so many things that I want to (and will) do, and I have to tell you that punching someone in the eye with a practiced right is not one of them. I never want to get into a fight again in my life, and if I have any say in it at all I won't. We sell ourselves short if we allow violence to define us, I refuse to be defined by something so grotesque. I choose better, I hope that you might too.

Animal Day is not easy, and it never will be. What I ask, is that you remember one thing: *if it were easy, everyone would be good*. Expect it to be hard, learn to handle hard by facing it as a way of life. If you expect it, anything less will be a bonus.

I have not added extra curriculum to this text, but it goes without saying that weights and anaerobic training, as an additive, will help you in your endeavour to improve. I have written books on all of the fighting distances that will help you immeasurably, *Watch My Back, Bouncer* and *On The Door* will show you the brutal reality of how it is on the pavement arena, my training books, *The Pavement Arena*, *Real Punching*, *Real Grappling*, *Real Kicking*, *Head, Knees & Elbows* and *Dead or Alive* will guide you to technical perfection and add a myriad of techniques to your curriculum. My book *Weight training - for the martial artist* will help develop the muscular strength and density to cope with the physical trauma of *all-out* and *Fear - the friend of exceptional people* will help you to understand, come to terms with and subsequently control fear. Besides that it is my recommendation that you devour as much data on the different fighting systems of the world as you can, make it, like I have, your life. Train with as many people and in as many systems as you can and experience the varying tastes of world martial arts. More than that, if you haven't already, take off the blinkers and see the world of combat in its true light, it is as ugly as it is immediate. If you are not attacking you'll be getting hit, if you're not first you'll be second and in the world of real, second place is last. With an enemy so brutal as the one we are now facing, last can mean DEAD!

Thank you for taking the time to read my book, I hope it has been of use. May your God bless you.